THE OAKWOOD LIBRARY OF RAILWAY H.

C000225946

Edwa

Thompson
of the
LNER

by
Peter Grafton

THE OAKWOOD PRESS

© Oakwood Press & Peter Grafton 2007

New Edition 2007
Originally published by Kestrel Books in 1971.

British Library Cataloguing in Publication Data
A Record for this book is available from the British Library
ISBN 978 0 85361 672 6

Typeset by Oakwood Graphics.
Repro by PKmediaworks, Cranborne, Dorset.
Printed by Cambrian Printers Ltd, Aberystwyth, an ISO14001 and Green Dragon
Level 5 certified printer on paper sourced from sustainable forests.

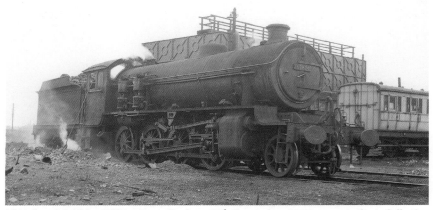

'O1' class 2-8-0 No. 63874 at Tyne Dock on 17th September, 1955.   *Author's Collection*

Title page: signed postcard view of LNER Pacific No. 500 *Edward Thompson*.

Front cover: 'St Margarets Sunset'. The end of another day at St Margarets shed in Edinburgh sees 'B1' 4-6-0 No. 61244 basking in the evening sun *circa* 1960. No. 61244 *Strang Steel* was, along with several other 'B1s', named after Directors of the LNER.
Philip D. Hawkins

Rear cover: The brooding presence of 'A2/2' Pacific No. 60506 *Wolf of Badenoch* lurks in the shed yard at New England, Peterborough waiting patiently for a spell of night duty *circa* 1960. This image is a detail from the painting 'Night Wolf'.   *Philip D. Hawkins*

To learn more about artist Philip D. Hawkins, his paintings, books and how to go about commissioning work, visit www.philipdhawkins.co.uk
For his Limited and Open Edition fine art prints visit www.quicksilverpublishing.co.uk

Published by The Oakwood Press (Usk), P.O. Box 13, Usk, Mon., NP15 1YS.
E-mail: sales@oakwoodpress.co.uk
Website: www.oakwoodpress.co.uk

Contents

	Preface to the New Edition	4
	Foreword to the First Edition *by C.F. Rose*	5
	Preface to the First Edition	6
Chapter One	Marlborough and Cambridge	7
Chapter Two	The Raven Influence	13
Chapter Three	Grouping and After	19
Chapter Four	Stratford 1927-1933	23
Chapter Five	Darlington 1934-1938	27
Chapter Six	Doncaster 1938-1941	35
Chapter Seven	The Years in Office 1941-1946	37
Chapter Eight	Retirement 1946-1954	131
Chapter Nine	The Final Analysis	135
	Epilogue	141
Appendix One	Summary of Thompson's Locomotive Work	142
Appendix Two	Locomotive Trials	143
Appendix Three	Names, Numbers and Dates	146
Appendix Four	Preservation	149
	Bibliography	151
	Index	151

'B1' class 4-6-0 No. 1248 *Geoffrey Gibbs*.   *Peter Townend Collection*

Preface to the New Edition

Over the years I have accumulated a plethora of information about Edward Thompson - some helpful and authoritative, some anecdotal. Much of this information has been incorporated in this edition and I feel that it presents a much more rounded picture of Thompson.

Once again I have been fortunate in the help and support that I have received during the preparation. It was the idea of Jane Kennedy of Oakwood Press and she has been wholeheartedly behind it: The Master of Marlborough College gave me unreserved access to the college archive and the archivist, Dr Terry Rogers was most helpful. As I have discovered over the years, the expertise and enthusiasm of the staff of the National Archive at Kew is invaluable.

Peter Townend read the text, made many helpful suggestions and provided photographs. Brian Stephenson of Rail Stephenson Archive was an invaluable source of images and spent many hours searching out photographs of Thompson-built locomotives as well as the many engines which he modified or rebuilt. I have quoted from various sources and they are acknowledged as appropriate in the text but should I have inadvertently forgotten anyone, I apologise. Sincere thanks are due to Dr Geoffrey Hughes and Richard Hardy for the help and assistance I received from them.

Finally, my thanks to my wife Sally. Without her enthusiasm - she acted as research assistant, critic and amanuensis - this edition would be incomplete.

Peter Grafton, 2007

Edward Thompson, 1881-1954.   *LNER*

Foreword to the First Edition

Insofar as any young man in the formative years of his career can be said to know his 'Chiefs' then I knew both Sir Nigel Gresley and Mr Edward Thompson. It would be idle to deny that there were many stories told in railway circles about these very different men that suggested that each had a deep-rooted dislike of the other.

All that I can say is that there was no definable evidence of this acrimony on one (awe-ful) occasion when Sir Nigel, visiting Stratford, sat at my drawing board discussing with Mr Thompson and the senior staff of the office details of a particular locomotive re-building, or indeed several years afterwards when Sir Nigel Gresley made frequent visits to Shildon works. Frequently on these occasions I was privileged to accompany Sir Nigel, Mr Thompson and Mr Cruddas as they walked around the works discussing the drastic changes already undertaken or contemplated at that works up to the time of Sir Nigel's death in harness, and this policy was continued vigorously by Mr Thompson, who may well have been the inspiration of it in any case. It is true to say that Mr Thompson had a great regard for Mr Cruddas, then the resident works manager (later to be works manager in his own right) at Shildon despite the fact that Sir Nigel had picked that very able man from outside industry and fostered him as something of a protégé at Doncaster, an almost unheard of happening in that age of railway history.

It would seem to temper the allegation that anyone favoured by Sir Nigel was automatically not acceptable to Mr Thompson. It is proper only to speak of a man from one's own experience. On that basis I must record that I received kindness from both men, but since my early years of training and work were spent in Stratford or Shildon, I had much greater opportunities to know Mr Thompson, and these increased during the five years Mr Thompson was chief mechanical engineer of the LNER. I was always impressed by Mr Thompson's erudite ability. His engineering decisions were clearly taken as a result of a logical study of the factors which had a bearing on the particular problem, and revealed an incisive clear-headedness. Although he seldom was patient enough to explain his own thinking, he would always listen as a contrary point of view was put before him; his decision was then made unequivocally clear.

When he succeeded Sir Nigel he told his senior officers 'I have so much to do, and only five years in which to do it'. This may well explain why some of his decisions seemed hasty, but anyone who studies where he had led as mechanical engineer will appreciate that he was well prepared to assume the responsibilities of chief mechanical engineer of the LNER and the output of his five years in that office tell of the prolific ideas he brought to light and implemented.

Mr Grafton's book will, I trust, do something to correct the long standing idea Mr Edward Thompson lived only for the opportunity to pull down what Sir Nigel had built up. I am glad that he has written it, believing as I do that Mr Thompson, albeit an academician, was also a trained engineer with a fund of good engineering sense in his own right, who reached his ultimate position of charge of an important department of a large railway company with a real sense of the urgency with which he must work if he was to accomplish what he wished to do before the date of his retirement came around.

C.F. Rose, B.Sc.(Eng.) C.Eng., F.I.Mech.E., F.I.Prod.E.,M.I.Loco.E.,
Executive Member, Central Engineering Training Group, British Railways Board

Preface to the First Edition

During the time that has been spent in the preparation of this book, I have travelled several hundred miles and interviewed many people who have given willingly of their time and hospitality, encouragement and support. I am particularly grateful to Mr C.F. Rose, upon whom I have leaned heavily and who has very kindly written the Foreword, to Stuart Rankin of the publishers for his confidence and his positive help, and to British Rail, Eastern Region.

Peter Townend, assistant divisional maintenance engineer, King's Cross, has been of tremendous help and I have passed many pleasant hours in his company. Mr F.G. Cockman of Bedford has been a veritable tower of strength, researching, encouraging and criticising, and vast quantities of 'midnight oil' have been burned in his study. Mr and Mrs Maurice Hall of Tunbridge Wells have a special place in this book - without their wholehearted co-operation it would be incomplete. They gave me unreserved access to many of Edward Thompson's personal possessions, as well as supplying much original information, and have read and approved the manuscript. Neil Clarke of Wellington and Philip Worner of Worcester College of Education have also read the manuscript and made many valuable and helpful suggestions, and much of the photographic material has come from the cameras of Peter Townend and my good friend Alan Thomas.

To the many former members of Thompson's staff, Miss Ivy Shingler, Messrs G.C. Gold, G.W. Taylor, C.F. Hinds, A.F. Cooper, W.S. Brooks and the late A.E. English, my thanks are due, as they are to those with whom I have corresponded but not met: Messrs E. Higginbottom and R.H. Inness. Information on the Thompson family background has been most generously supplied and checked by Mr Oliver Carter of Wigtown and by Edward Thompson's cousin, Mr Guy L. Thompson, F.R.C.S. of Hutton-le-Hole.

The established authors have been generous in allowing me to quote freely from their works and in supplying information. I am indebted in this respect to Messrs Cecil J. Allen, O.S. Nock, K. Hoole and W.B. Yeadon.

Finally to my wife Sally, a special word of thanks. Without her patient understanding and forbearance - not always easy with three young children demanding attention - the book would never have been started.

Peter Grafton
Paignton, Devon
November 1970

Chapter One

Marlborough and Cambridge

At a ceremony held at Marylebone station on 31st May, 1946, the Chairman of the LNER, Sir Ronald Matthews, removed the covers from the nameplates of one of the company's new Pacific locomotives and bestowed on it the name of its designer, *Edward Thompson.*

This simple act, performed with the minimum of publicity and fuss, marked the end of Thompson's five years as chief mechanical engineer (CME) of the LNER and the end of almost 45 years in railway service. He officially retired on 30th June, 1946, and went to his retirement confident in the knowledge that he had interpreted the requirements of his office during the years of World War II as he thought best. He paid little heed to his critics - of whom there were many - and forged ahead, making decisions and having the strength of character to stand by them.

Edward Thompson died in 1954. Since then, and with gathering momentum the rights and wrongs of his actions during his years as chief mechanical engineer have been debated and some 50 years later, the debate continues.

It is safe to state that no other chief mechanical engineer has been the subject of so much speculation, criticism and downright denigration, and yet through it all, Thompson the man remains, quite characteristically, something of an enigma. He did not have the breadth of vision of his eminent predecessor, Sir Nigel Gresley, nor the unorthodox enterprise of his contemporary, O.V.S. Bullied CME of the Southern Railway. But these are negative qualities; what did Thompson have that was positive? This book attempts to answer that question.

Born at Marlborough College on 25th June, 1881, Thompson was the youngest of a family of four and was the only boy. His father, Francis Edward, was a Scholar of Lincoln College, Oxford and was awarded a First Class Degree in Classics, proceeding to an MA in 1860. He was a notable Greek scholar and in his later years wrote and published Greek textbooks. He joined the staff of Marlborough in 1859 having previously taught in a private school where he succeeded to the class taken by R.D. Blackmore. In 1861 he became Housemaster of B2 house and, as was the custom at the time, he relinquished the house on his marriage in 1869 but was back in charge of Cotton House in 1872.

Marlborough School was founded by the Revd Charles Plater in 1842 as a school for the sons of the clergy, and became Marlborough College under a charter dated 1845. Its history between 1843 and 1858 is, to say the least, chequered, but reforms were started by the Revd G.E.L. Cotton, who became Headmaster in 1852. Amongst the reforms were the building of up-to-date accommodation to the designs of the eminent Victorian ecclesiastical architect, George Edmund Street and to be designated Cotton and Littlefield Houses. F.E. Thompson was involved in the designs and it was felt to be appropriate that he should be the first Housemaster of Cotton House. According to an obituary published in *The Marlburian* in March 1916, 'As first master and maker of Cotton House, he [F.E. Thompson] counts directly as one of the creators of

Littlefield House, Marlborough College, 1899. Edward Thompson, with arms folded, is on the left of housemaster Henry Richardson.

Marlborough College teaching staff in 1890. F.E. Thompson, bearded, stands tall and proud, as he stares into the distance from the middle of the back row.

Marlborough'. The building of the houses was not without incident. It is assumed that Street was commissioned to carry out the work because of his connection with the Established Church and the buildings are, by Victorian standards, austere. No doubt Street was expected to keep costs to a minimum and the correspondence between Street and the College authorities reveals that he complained regularly, one example being the cost of clearing the site at $4\frac{1}{2}d$. per wagon load. In due course the buildings were completed and, in 1858, Cotton received his preferment and was consecrated Bishop of Calcutta. Unfortunately, in the course of his pastoral duties as he was boarding a boat on the River Hooghly he slipped, fell into the river and was drowned.

Cotton was succeeded by Revd G.G. Bradley who was a pupil at Rugby at the time that Thomas Arnold was Headmaster. After university he joined the teaching staff at Rugby and became a housemaster. He was specifically nominated for the Headship of Marlborough by Cotton in 1858 and during his 12 years' tenure of office put the school firmly on the road to the eminent position it occupies today. His ability as a Headmaster and a teacher was held in high esteem by staff and school alike, and there is little doubt that under his influence and personality, Francis Edward Thompson's views, ideals and sense of values were formulated. At any rate, he spent all his teaching life at Marlborough, and remained connected with it, later as a Governor, until his death in 1916.

The Thompson family history shows artistic, academic and commercial successes, leavened, as befits an English family, with the sea. Captain John Bailey, RN, Thompson's great-great-grandfather, sailed from Dartmouth to Canada, was captured by Montcalm in the St Lawrence and released by General Wolfe after the successful storming of the Heights of Abraham.

His great-grandfather ran a flourishing tailoring business in Conduit Street, London, and his grandfather, Francis, was an accomplished artist and architect as well as being a successful businessman and he was closely associated with George and Robert Stephenson. He invested heavily in railways and designed railway stations on the North Midland and Chester & Holyhead railways, Chester being the outstanding example. He was a man of considerable means and seems to have followed architecture as a hobby, although he obviously received very sound training.

The sea also figured in Francis Thompson's life as he was very fond of Dartmouth and for many years had a yacht berthed there. Following his death, the family business passed to his second son, the Revd R.W. Thompson who realised his ambition by entering the Church and having done so, disposed of the business in 1881. Under the patronage of Baroness Burdett Coutts, a member of the banking family and a close friend of the Thompsons, he became chaplain at the Chapel Royal, Savoy, London.

Here, then we have Edward Thompson growing up against the background of Victorianism at its best - or worst - the ultra middle-class environment of what was becoming an important public school, a father who was very much part of the hierarchy within the school, the corporate life of which was a microcosm of the class structure as it was at the time. As a child of a member of staff, he would constantly be under surveillance and whatever his natural tendencies might have been, they would have to be curbed in order to suit his surroundings. Children were not heard and, if a suitable governess could be found, were only seen at certain times. Added to this, Francis Thompson was approaching middle-age at the time of his son's birth and he doubtless held very marked views on what was good for children in general, and boys in particular. (In Edward's case, a suitable governess was found. She was French by birth and under her influence he became almost bilingual and spoke French fluently.)

Thompson once remarked that he felt that he was a disappointment to his father, who knew little of mechanical engineering and never really understood why his son wanted to make it his career. There was a strong Oxford tradition in the family and with it there was a classics tradition. Edward Thompson broke with both of these to go up to Cambridge to read Mechanical Sciences.

Little is known of Mrs Francis Edward Thompson, other than that she and her son were very close. She appears to have organized her daughters and her household to cater for her son's needs when he returned to Marlborough during his holidays, and it seems that her marriage was happy by the standards of the time. Following her husband's death in 1916, she was a frequent visitor to her son's home until her death in 1925.

At the age of eight, Edward Thompson was sent to St David's School, Reigate, a preparatory school geared to educating its pupils for Common Entrance. His career seems to have been uneventful and he played cricket for the school. This no doubt stimulated his interest in individual ball games, as later in life he became an extremely good golfer.

His early years in Marlborough and his journeys to and from Reigate, travelling part of the journey behind Brunel's broad gauge locomotives, may well have influenced him in his choice of career and one likes to think of him taking a keen interest in the final conversion to standard gauge in 1892. Here is a curious parallel with the early life of Sir Nigel Gresley with whom Thompson was associated for so many years - Gresley was educated at Marlborough and was there towards the close of the broad gauge era.

From St David's, Thompson returned to Marlborough joining upper fourth form A at Easter 1895 and was in Henry Richardson's Littlefield House. He was now more than a staff child, he was a pupil, and he probably found himself in the invidious position of having to subjugate his feelings and opinions in order to avoid casting any adverse reflection on his father's position in the school.

Marlborough College archive contains details of Thompson's progress between 1895 and 1899 - academically he was not a high flyer. His first report shows that he came 20th out of 27 in form A, although he had made some progress by the end of his second term being placed eighth out of 29. From then on his academic attainments were only average and at the end of his time at Marlborough - summer 1899 - he was 17th out of 21 in the engineering class.

Away from the classroom and workshop, Thompson was in his element. Apart from being a Dormitory Captain he was in House teams for rugby, gymnastics, tug of war and cricket and in addition he was placed first in the drop kick competition two years in succession. He went on to play rugby for the school first XV but cricket was his main sport. Despite the fact that his backstroke was judged to be weak, he was in the first XI and played in a two-day match against Rugby School at Lord's in 1899. The team was captained by R.H. Spooner and Marlborough won handsomely. Spooner, who scored 198 out of 318 in the second innings, went on to play for Lancashire and in 10 test matches for England between 1905 and 1912.

In 1899 Thompson went up to Pembroke College, Cambridge to read Mechanical Sciences and in 1902 he took the Final Examinations in the Mechanical Sciences Tripos, being awarded a Class 3 degree. This was noted in *The Marlburian* of 28th July, 1902 along with degrees awarded by Pembroke to seven other Old Marlburians.

At this point in his life, on the threshold of his career, Thompson seems to have been a conscientious and hard-working young man and certainly not the man who, in the minds of many, stands accused and indicted of attempting to undo all that Gresley had done before him.

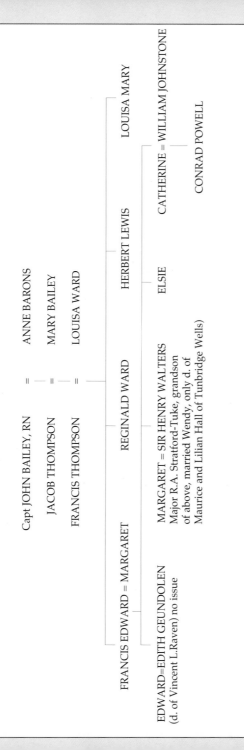

Capt JOHN BAILEY, RN = ANNE BARONS

JACOB THOMPSON = MARY BAILEY

FRANCIS THOMPSON = LOUISA WARD

FRANCIS EDWARD = MARGARET | REGINALD WARD | HERBERT LEWIS | LOUISA MARY

EDWARD=EDITH GEUNDOLEN
(d. of Vincent L.Raven) no issue

MARGARET = SIR HENRY WALTERS
Major R.A. Stratford-Tuke, grandson
of above, married Wendy, only d. of
Maurice and Lilian Hall of Tunbridge Wells)

ELSIE

CATHERINE = WILLIAM JOHNSTONE

CONRAD POWELL

Abstract from Thompson family tree prepared from information provided by Mrs S.C. Gardner and Mr Guy L. Thompson FRCS, both of whom were grandchildren of Reginald Ward Thompson and second cousins of Edward Thompson.

Chapter Two

The Raven Influence

From Cambridge, Thompson joined Beyer, Peacock & Co. Ltd, at Manchester as a pupil in the drawing office. Apart from this, and the dates of his appointment and resignation, there is nothing in the company's records that refers to him, and so it can only be assumed that he worked on locomotive design and gained experience of drawing office practice.

Thompson left Manchester and in 1904 went to the Midland Railway at Derby, the year after R.M. Deeley had succeeded S.W. Johnson as chief mechanical engineer. The works manager was Cecil Paget, for whom Thompson developed great admiration and, when he - Thompson - arrived at Derby, exciting things were happening, not the least of which were the designs for the 'Paget Locomotive'. Paget - later Sir Cecil - was a brilliant engineer and in attempting to introduce a locomotive that was revolutionary both in design and concept, he anticipated by nearly 40 years another brilliant engineer, O.V.S. Bulleid.

The Paget locomotive had 2-6-2 wheel arrangement with eight single-acting cylinders of 18 in. diameter and 12 in. stroke, arranged in two groups of four, each group formed from a single casting. Perhaps its most remarkable innovation was the valve gear, which consisted of rotary sleeve valves, then very much in vogue on stationary steam engines. This attempt by Paget to introduce sleeve valves on a locomotive was not repeated until Bulleid's ill-fated 'Leader' of 1946. Other unusual features were a firebox that was simply a brick lined furnace with a pair of fire doors at one end and a steel plate at the other, the whole totally devoid of copper, and a smokebox hopper.

Although the locomotive did not run on its initial trials until 1908, patents were taken out by Paget for the cylinder layout and the valve year in 1904 and 1905 respectively, at which time Thompson was closely associated with him. The two men became friends, a friendship that lasted until Paget's death in 1936. The Paget locomotive attained a speed of 83 mph during trials and on the occasion of its final run the valves seized solid at 70 mph. (For full details see *The British Steam Locomotive 1825-1925*, E.L. Ahrons.)

Thompson was with the Midland for nearly two years, during which time he worked as an improver in Derby sheds as well as gaining experience in various departments, and had his first taste of life on the shop floor.

In 1905 he moved to Woolwich Arsenal, but by 1906 was back in the railway world, this time joining the North Eastern Railway (NER) at Hull Dairycoates as assistant to the locomotive superintendent, Bill Farrow.

Thompson spent the years at Hull learning the practicalities of locomotive working, and in 1909 was transferred to Gateshead as assistant to the Northern running superintendent, the redoubtable 'Charlie' Baister, whose son, S.L. Baister, was, in later years, works manager at Stratford under Thompson.

There is no doubt that Wilson Worsdell, then CME of the NER, was aware of Thompson's ability and moved him to Gateshead, where the company's headquarters were situated. In 1910 Worsdell retired and was succeeded by his assistant, Vincent Raven.

Painstaking research spread over nearly three years failed to reveal precisely how or why Thompson decided upon a railway career. It is possible that during his undergraduate days Thompson met Norman Raven - Vincent Raven's elder son - and was introduced to the family.

Raven senior may well have had a quick appreciation of Thompson's potential and may have suggested that railways would offer him a satisfying and worthwhile future. He probably mapped out the steps and used his influence to set Thompson upon the road that eventually led to Gateshead in 1909. One thing is certain, as assistant CME of a large and prosperous railway company, Vincent Raven would be in contact with the senior staff of Beyer, Peacock, of Deeley and Paget at Derby and, of course, of Wilson Worsdell. Raven also had connections with Woolwich Arsenal.

Admittedly, the foregoing is supposition, but in considering Thompson's early career, the supposition is not unreasonable. In 1913, Thompson's connections with the Raven family became closer, for on 25th June - his 32nd birthday - he married Vincent Raven's younger daughter, Guendolen, at Holy Trinity Church, Darlington. Judging from reports in the local paper - *The North Star* - the wedding was one of the highlights of the Darlington social season. The paper was somewhat excessive in its reporting of the event, 17 lines of a two inch column

Sir Vincent Raven.   Mrs Edward Thompson, 1937 (née Guen
                    Mr & Mrs M.H. Hall   Raven).   *Mr & Mrs M.H. Hall*

being devoted to a description of the bride's dress. Every guest was listed - and these ranged from Col Sir Charles Allan to Master Roger Gresley - as was every wedding present. Included amongst the latter were a revolving bookcase from Mr and Mrs H.N. Gresley and an 'old' table from Mr and Mrs W. Worsdell (it is assumed that the table was antique.) Norman Raven was the best man and Violet Gresley was one of the four bridesmaids. The reception was held at the bride's home and the honeymoon was spent in Paris and Switzerland.

Although Raven influenced Thompson's career with its various moves, he had little influence on life away from work. Raven was a 'clubbable' man: a Freemason, JP, local councillor and vice-Chairman of Governors, Darlington Technical College and obviously very community-minded. Similarly, Lady Raven was involved in the community being, amongst other things, President of Darlington WI. Thompson senior was involved with the community in which he lived. Apart from his dedication to the school, he embraced the cause of Liberalism, first in the Parliamentary Borough of Marlborough and then in the East Wiltshire division. On his retirement he moved to London and served on Hampstead Borough Council for 10 years, In addition he was on the council of the Hellenic Society, and was on the Boards of several secondary schools. He played golf until he was 80 and on giving up the game joined the local Horticultural Society. In spite of two splendid role models, Edward Thompson tended to be solitary in his away-from-work interests. He was an accomplished cabinet maker and he had a deep and lasting interest in history. He played golf regularly, usually with Norman Raven (and that involved only one other person) and occasionally making up a foursome with the Ravens senior and junior and Arthur Stamer - people with whom he was comfortable. As far as can be ascertained, Thompson's one and only involvement with the community was when he served for a short time on the management committee of Darlington Memorial Hospital. It is rumoured that on hearing that there were plans to provide radios for the patients he commented: 'Wireless - these people should count themselves lucky to have beds'. If this is indeed true, and perhaps it wouldn't be too far out of character, little wonder that his association with the hospital was brief.

If Thompson and Raven had differing attitudes towards involvement in the community, they were on the same wave length when it came to labour relations. Raven's attitude towards the work force left much to be desired as is reflected in his diaries. His finest hour came in December 1912 when he precipitated a strike over what became known as 'The Right to get Drunk'. This was a *cause celebre* that involved the demotion of Nichol Knox, a driver with 37 years' service with the NER and an unblemished record, for - allegedly - being drunk and disorderly some 30 hours before he was due on duty. Raven's action and attitude had the unions up in arms, baying for his head on a salver. Eventually Knox was granted a Royal Pardon. (For full details, see the author's *Sir Vincent Raven and the North Eastern Railway*, Oakwood Press.)

Whilst Thompson was not embroiled in the Knox affair, he was engaged to Guen Raven - their wedding was a mere six months away - and he must have been aware of the situation. In all probability he discussed it over the port with his putative father-in-law and if indeed this happened, then Thompson did not learn from Raven's experience. That he - Thompson - did not precipitate a strike was probably more by luck than by judgement because his handling of staff and trades union officials was deplorable. He had no idea how to be diplomatic and his autocratic bearing did not endear him to his own staff in general or to his workshop staff. 'Freddie' Harrison (Robin Riddles' second in command) expands on this aspect of Thompson's attitude: '…this created many managerial difficulties which his staff, unbeknown to him, had to be smoothed over and try to protect him from the consequences' and with masterly understatement, Harrison concludes, 'This aspect of his character cannot be counted as a plus value'.

Shortly after succeeding Worsdell, Vincent Raven visited the USA to study at first hand the various electrification schemes that were being undertaken by several American railway companies.

Raven was a strong advocate of electrification and had plans for its introduction on the line between Shildon and Tees (Newport) Yards. He proposed an overhead supply system with locomotives of his own design and had plans for the electrification of the whole of the main line between Newcastle and York and had gained experience of the running problems associated with electric traction on the Newcastle suburban services. Amongst the party of NER officials that accompanied him were A.C. Stamer and Edward Thompson.

In 1911, with the completion of the company's new offices in Brinkburn Road, Darlington, the CME's staff was moved from Gateshead. Thompson stayed behind and continued to work under Baister until 1912 when he left the NER and joined the Great Northern Railway (GNR) as carriage & wagon superintendent at Doncaster. Immediately one is faced with the question, why did he move to another company when things seemed set fair with the NER? His friendship with the Ravens was very firm and his marriage to Guen Raven was planned.

It seems likely that Thompson was acutely aware of his position *vis-à-vis* the Ravens and the NER, and felt that it would be unwise to 'marry the boss's daughter'. Up to the time that he moved to Doncaster, his carriage and wagon experience was limited and so he took the opportunity to go to the GNR when a vacancy arose. His administrative ability had made its mark and no doubt Raven recommended him to Gresley on this particular point. Although this may have had the suggestion of nepotism, it would be less likely to provoke adverse comment than would a comparable promotion within the framework of the NER. Thus, Thompson went to Doncaster and began an association with the works that spanned, with one or two breaks, 34 years.

He is remembered during his early days at Doncaster for his attempts to create a good impression and to settle into his new job, his immaculate dress - always important - his consideration for some of his staff, his generosity and his helpfulness in engineering matters, particularly in the drawing office. He is also remembered, somewhat significantly in the light of subsequent development, for his absolute insistence that all should be tidy.

Whilst at Doncaster Thompson played cricket for the works XI and on the occasion of the opening of the pavilion at Darlington Railway Athletic Ground, he captained a Great Northern Railway team in a match against a North Eastern Railway team captained by A.C. Stamer. In this celebration game the NER won by 18 runs, Thompson's contribution to the GNR total of 95 being only 2 before he was bowled. He was, however, last man in. Perhaps his backstroke continued to be weak?

Thompson's regard for the Ravens is reflected in the naming of his house in Thorne Road, Doncaster. It was called Litchfield, a Raven family name. From here he was married and it was here that Edward and Guen Thompson set up home together.

The first year of their marriage was well-ordered and reflected a mode of life that was common to most upper middle class families. The pages of Mrs Thompson's visitors' book show that entertaining played an important part in her life, and judging from the comment written by Francis Thompson, 'Filially entertained. *Quid plura?*' the standard of comfort at 'Litchfield' was excellent. In *Thompson and Peppercorn Locomotive Engineers* (Ian Allan 1979) Col H.C.B. Rogers suggests that the Thompsons' marriage was not wholly successful. In an otherwise meticulously annotated book, Col Rogers does not give a source for the statement. There is, however, more than a grain of truth in it. Whilst researching for the First Edition, it became clear that Thompson had an eye for the ladies - he was no Lothario - but he had a weakness for a pretty face - and it was hinted that he had two extra-marital affairs, probably over-lapping. At the time that the First Edition was published, it would have been very unwise to name names and even now it is perhaps as well to let sleeping ladies lie.

But the end of an era was rapidly approaching and was marked by the assassination of Archduke Franz Ferdinand in June 1914. Following the invasion of Belgium by Germany some two months later, the British Government took the necessary powers to deal with the situation, the pattern of life changed for everyone and the lights did indeed go out all over Europe.

In May 1915, Vincent Raven was seconded to Government Service as Chief Superintendent of the Royal Ordnance Factory, Woolwich, and A.C. Stamer was appointed to take over as acting CME of the NER. In 1916 Thompson joined his father-in-law and once again found himself at Woolwich, although he did not stay long before going to France to join the staff of the Director General of Transportation, the ubiquitous Eric Geddes. A multi-talented and a quite remarkable man, Geddes held senior rank in the army and navy, was an MP, was Minister of Transport in Lloyd George's coalition Government and he was one of the architects of the Railways Act 1921. He it was who insisted that 'North Eastern Railway' was incorporated in the title of the new London & North Eastern Railway (LNER). He joined the NER in 1904 and such were his talents that he quickly rose to be Deputy General Manager and he fully expected to succeed Sir Alexander Butterworth as General Manager. World War I, however, had a dramatic effect on Geddes's future as noted above and having shaped the 1921 Act, he fancied his chances of becoming the first Chairman of the LNER. Unfortunately, Geddes had upset too many people and the NER severed all connection with him with a £50,000 pay off. This caused controversy and questions were asked in Parliament. The outcome was that Sir Frederick Banbury - Chairman of the GNR - and William Whitelaw, supported by Walter K. Whigham, would have nothing to do with Geddes, and William Whitelaw, former Chairman of the North British Railway was appointed Chairman of the LNER from 1st January, 1923. Geddes was knighted for his services during World War I but is probably best remembered for his re-organizing of the civil service after the war. The changes that he proposed were so far-reaching and drastic that it was said at the time that he wielded the 'Geddes axe'. In 1917 Vincent Raven was knighted for his services and became Deputy Controller of Armament Production at the Admiralty.

Unfortunately, the War Office has been unable to provide full details of Thompson's war record. He was mostly concerned with large-scale movements of troops, was twice mentioned in dispatches and was demobilised in 1919 with the rank of Lieut-Colonel. For his wartime services, Thompson was appointed an Officer the Order of the British Empire, Military Division.

Thompson returned to civilian life and to the GNR at Doncaster, but stayed only a year before going back to the NER as carriage & wagon manager at York. During that year, Gresley's first quintuplet articulated coach set was under construction at Doncaster. Incorporated in the five-coach train was an all-electric kitchen car which was self-contained but which could be adapted to use mains supply at terminal stations. It was built for use on the Kings Cross-Leeds run, and although Thompson was associated with the set he moved to York before it was completed. The move - which can be construed at best as a sideways move - was no doubt prompted by the prospect of The Railways Act 1921. Thompson felt that when the proposed legislation became law, as a member of the Raven family, he ought to be where its influence was greatest – with the North Eastern Railway.

His work as carriage & wagon works manager was largely concerned with administration, planning and the managing of a large work force. He did little, if any, designing, but he did contribute in a very marked way to the efficiency of the operation of the works.

Mass production, as we know it today was virtually unheard of in the early 1920s, although Henry Ford's methods of car production were steadily gaining ground. The continuous conveyor system of vehicle assembly was replacing laborious hand-built methods, particularly in the manufacture of cheap models.

Thompson was impressed with Ford's ideas and argued that if they could be adapted to the construction of railway passenger vehicles, costs might be reduced and production increased. He spent a long time planning a system that could be introduced at York carriage works with the minimum of interference to production, and his final scheme was elaborately worked out on his desk, using matchsticks and matchboxes to represent the stages in the construction of coaches. His system was eventually adopted and York carriage & wagon works became very well known for its building methods. Visitors came from all over Europe and Thompson commented on several occasions that he could not carry on with his routine work for entertaining them and conducting them around the works.

In the meantime, he kept in touch with all that was happening at Darlington. Although the Thompsons continued to live in Doncaster, Sir Vincent and Lady Raven visited them frequently and Thompson was a close friend of Sir Vincent's deputy A.C. Stamer. Thus, he was very much aware of North Eastern Railway policy, particularly with regard to locomotive matters and there must have been some tension as Vesting Day for the 1921 Act approached.

Chapter Three

Grouping and After

The Railways' Act of 1921 that became effective on 1st January, 1923 provided for the amalgamation of the country's many independent railways into four main companies: the London, Midland & Scottish Railway (LMS), the London & North Eastern Railway, the Great Western Railway (GWR), and the Southern Railway.

The formation of the major networks was, for want of a better expression, a cross between nationalisation and take-over. Whilst on the one hand it was enforced by statute, the new companies were theoretically free from Government interference; they were run by a Chairman and Directors drawn from the Boards of constituent companies and responsible to the shareholders. The London & North Eastern Railway was formed by the amalgamation of the North Eastern Railway, the North British Railway, the Great Northern Railway, the Great Central Railway, the Great North of Scotland Railway, the Great Eastern Railway (GER) and some minor companies. There had been some 'mini-grouping' before 1923, when, for instance, the Hull & Barnsley Railway was absorbed by the North Eastern Railway.

Having settled the question of who was to be the first Chairman of the new company, the Directors turned their attention to the appointment of its first chief mechanical engineer.

J.G. Robinson, chief mechanical engineer of the Great Central Railway, Sir Vincent Raven, chief mechanical engineer of the North Eastern Railway, and H.N. Gresley of the Great Northern Railway were undoubtedly favourites. Robinson had been chief mechanical engineer of the Great Central Railway since 1900 and was very much the elder statesman of all of the constituent companies. He had made his mark on early 20th century locomotive design and practice with his 4-4-0 'Director' class and he was a very experienced engineer. He was, however, approaching 70 and rumour has it that he was offered the appointment, but declined because of his age.

Sir Vincent Raven was appointed chief mechanical engineer of the North Eastern Railway in 1910 - at about the same time that Gresley was appointed to the Great Northern Railway - and the North Eastern Railway was, at the time of Grouping, the largest, richest and perhaps the most influential of the constituent companies. It had a monopoly of freight traffic in the North East and was regarded as progressive and go ahead although its detractors regarded it as a provincial company because there was no London terminus. When, for example, several elephants had to be transported from Newcastle to Manchester, the North Eastern Railway promptly designed and built elephant vans for the purpose!

Raven was a strong protagonist of electrification and worked extremely hard to put the North Eastern Railway ahead of its competitors in the use of electric traction. In 1904 electric shunters were introduced in Trafalgar Yard, Newcastle, and, following Raven's visit to the USA in 1911, his proposals for the electrification of the Shildon-Tees (Newport) Yard line were accepted and finally approved in 1913. The system operated at 1.5kV with overhead pick-up. Ten locomotives were built to Raven's designs and the line became fully operational in July 1916.

Raven quickly followed this with an 18-page report to his Directors, putting forward a very strong case for the electrification of the main line from York to Newcastle. He proposed a dual-system, third-rail and catenary, operating at 1.5 kV. His closely reasoned arguments, quoting both installation and maintenance costs, make this document, dated October 1919, extremely interesting reading. Twelve years later, the Weir Committee reported on its investigations into electrification of the country's railways as a whole and echoed many of the points that had been put forward by Sir Vincent Raven.

Apart from this, he had designed several successful classes of steam locomotives, perhaps the best known being his 'Z' class Atlantics, although his 'S3s' (later 'B16s') survived almost to the end of steam.

H.N. Gresley succeeded H.A. Ivatt as locomotive superintendent of the Great Northern Railway in 1911, at the incredibly early age of 35. He, too, had made his mark on locomotive development by producing a series of designs in a comparatively short period of time. These range from his 0-6-2 tank engines, his three-cylinder 2-6-0 engines to the three 4-6-2 Pacifics that were built just before Grouping. His sphere of influence extended beyond locomotives, as he had shown himself to be a very good designer of rolling stock. Gresley was comparatively young at the time of Grouping and he was enterprising and liberal in his approach to his job.

At the time that speculation was rife, Thompson had been carriage & wagon works manager at York for three years, years that were both pleasant and profitable. He had left the Great Northern Railway in 1920 to return to the North Eastern Railway and was, by now, a North Eastern man. He was working under the direction of A.C. Stamer who as mechanical engineer was Sir Vincent Raven's deputy.

Had Sir Vincent Raven become chief mechanical engineer of the London and North Eastern Railway, he would have retired in 1927. In all probability he would have been succeeded by Gresley who, as chief mechanical engineer of 11 years' standing prior to Grouping, would undoubtedly have been appointed as Raven's assistant.

Continuing the speculation, A.C. Stamer might have become Gresley's assistant, and on Stamer's retirement in 1933, it is fair to assume that Thompson would have succeeded him. Having occupied a senior position on two of the major companies that were absorbed by the LNER, Thompson might reasonably expect promotion and might reasonably have expected Gresley to retire on reaching the age of 60 in 1936, after having been CME for almost 25 years.

The realities, and subsequent history of the LNER, are, however, very different from speculation. The Directors of the newly formed railway decreed that its chief mechanical engineer must be based at King's Cross and Sir Vincent Raven let it be known that he was not prepared to move - neither he nor Lady Raven had any wish to leave the North East (Lady Raven in particular) and yet when Sir Vincent finally severed all connections with the railway world in 1927 he and Lady Raven moved to Hook in Hampshire. Thus, the appointment went to Gresley, who we are told was strongly supported by J.G. Robinson. Sir Vincent Raven was retained by the LNER on a consultant basis for one year.

Although the appointment of Gresley must have been a disappointment to Thompson and his wife, for they were both fond of Sir Vincent, Mrs Thompson being particularly close to him, the future must still have looked bright. For reasons already stated, Thompson could expect promotion, and in the troubled post-war years, railway service offered far more security than industry and offered a very reasonable salary to people in senior positions. At about this time, for instance, W.A. Stanier, later Sir William, was earning £500 per year. He later explained that this was sufficient to keep a wife, a car, and a parlour maid. On the other hand, R.L. Wedgwood was appointed Chief General Manager of the newly-formed LNER at a salary of £10,000.

Thompson might have felt that had there been friction of any sort during the formative years of the LNER he was well supported by Sir Vincent Raven who undoubtedly had close contact with several of the Directors and with the newly-appointed Chief General Manager.

The formation of the LNER came at a time when the country was in the throes of both social and economic upheaval. Industrial unrest was centred on the mining industry and the failure of Lloyd George's administration to carry out its wartime promise of nationalisation. There was to a certain extent an aura of uncertainty, yet in spite of this, Thompson's professional status improved. He was appointed carriage & wagon engineer for the entire North Eastern area of the LNER and although this was a similar job to that which he had been doing before Grouping he now had increased responsibility and a greater degree of mobility. Some of his North Eastern friends also received promotion - A.C. Stamer became chief assistant mechanical engineer based at Darlington (he subsequently became assistant chief mechanical engineer) and F.W. Wintour was brought from Darlington works to Doncaster as assistant mechanical engineer, Southern Area of the LNER.

Thompson continued with the work that he had started at York in 1920 and increased his experience of administration, organization and methods. During the period under review, LNER development policy was centred on locomotives, with Gresley promulgating his big engine policy. He continued to build his Pacifics and 1925 was the year of the LNER/GWR locomotive exchanges, the background to which is given in C.J. Allen's *The Locomotive Exchanges*. The lessons that Gresley learned from the exchanges had a far-reaching effect on Pacific design and although Thompson was not directly concerned, the results no doubt stood him in good stead in later years.

Another highlight of 1925 was the celebrations to mark the centenary of the opening of the Stockton & Darlington Railway, the main event of which was a locomotive pageant that showed the evolution of locomotive and carriage design. The exhibits ranged from *Locomotion*, hauling a rake of chaldron wagons with passengers in period costume, to Gresley's latest creation, the 2-8-8-2 Beyer-Garratt locomotive. Stands were erected in a lineside field at Fighting Cocks, outside Darlington, and the impressive panorama of 53 exhibits moved slowly past the official guests and the public, who turned out in hundreds to see what was a memorable show. A.C.Stamer was responsible for this masterpiece of organization and planning, which not only involved the preparation of the LNER's exhibits but also arrangements to have representatives of other companies' locomotives in the right place at the right time. He was ably assisted by Thompson who was responsible for the organization of the exhibits at Stockton where they were shedded prior to moving in procession to Fighting Cocks.

Whilst Stamer and his team were busy arranging the celebrations, the country's industrial climate was slowly deteriorating. Unemployment was high and there had been three governments between 1921 and 1924, none of which seemed capable of tackling the problem. By 1924 the mining industry was feeling the effects of German and Polish competition in overseas markets and British coalowners were not prepared to invest profits in modernising the mines. In fact, they demanded a longer working day with a reduction in wages. A Royal Commission was appointed to study the mining industry and it reported in March 1926 recommending nationalisation and modernisation with a reduction in pay. This was rejected by the miners, led by Herbert Smith and A.J. Cook, and on 1st May, 1926 they went on strike. This was followed three days later by the General Strike which included workers in transport and heavy industry.

As with many services, the railways were kept running by a miscellaneous corps of volunteers, managed by non-strikers and administrative staff and so, after an absence of several years, Thompson was back on the operating side. But the General Strike was a nine days' wonder and although the miners stayed out for several months, they eventually returned to work.

Against this background, Thompson's life changed very little. His job was secure, he was well paid by the standards of the time and life at 'Litchfield' was far removed from the realities of the mid-1920s. Friendships formed in the days before the war continued - Mr & Mrs (later Sir Ronald and Lady) Matthews and the Kitsons of the Leeds engineering firm were amongst frequent visitors to Doncaster and his friendship with his brother-in-law Norman Raven continued.

Thompson suffered a great personal loss with the death of his mother in 1925. As has already been remarked, they were very close and she had always been concerned about his welfare. During his bachelor days in Darlington she had frequently stayed with him and during the years following her husband's death in 1916 she spent some time with the Thompsons at 'Litchfield'.

In 1927 as the country was trying to recover from the effects of the General Strike and was moving inexorably towards the depression, Thompson's career took a significant upward turn when he was appointed assistant mechanical engineer at Stratford under C.W.L. Glaze.

Chapter Four

Stratford 1927-1933

During the first three years at Stratford, Thompson was concerned with works organization, particularly at Temple Mills wagon works, Glaze being quick to make use of his - Thompson's - carriage and wagon experience.

The *Railway Magazine* for March 1930 noted the retirement of Glaze and the appointment of Thompson to succeed him. Glaze had been mechanical engineer, Stratford since 1923 and had a railway career that dated from 1885 when he joined the Great Eastern Railway at the age of 15. He was an experienced engineer and very much 'hands on' - a hard act to follow. Thompson was not the man to be overawed by a predecessor and he relished the opportunity of being responsible for Stratford.

His appointment coincided with the retirement from Doncaster of F. Wintour. The two men were friendly and would occasionally spend a weekend playing golf at Felixstowe, sometimes accompanied by A.C. Stamer and Sir Vincent Raven. Felixstowe golf course was Raven's favourite and he played there as often as he could.

Thompson was as keen as ever on the game and he applied himself with characteristic determination to reducing his handicap. His interest in cricket also continued and he encouraged the works' team at Stratford.

It was at about this time that the former Great Eastern Railway Company's Directors' Scholarships were re-introduced. There was always a strong education tradition at Stratford dating from the foundation of the Great Eastern Mechanics Institute in West Ham in 1851. Qualified staff were released from their duties in the works for a given time each week to lecture in the Institute, which was under the control of a part-time principal appointed from the works, and a full time administrative officer.

Gresley was never particularly interested in the educational side of railway work and was reluctant to accept the re-introduction of the Directors' Scholarships, but he yielded to pressure from William Whitelaw, Chairman of the company. The Great Eastern had given six awards annually - Gresley recommended that the same figure should apply to the whole of the LNER.

Thompson, who always encouraged the work of the staff and students at the Mechanics' Institute, was particularly pleased when three of the six awards made in the year of the re-introduction were gained by Stratford apprentices. The awards were tenable at East London College, which later became Queen Mary College, a constituent college of London University.

In connection with the Directors' Scholars, two incidents that occurred clearly illustrate Thompson's character.

One of the Directors' Scholars, C.F. Rose, was secretary of the College Engineering Society and had arranged for Gresley to lecture to the members. Thompson was present and was introduced to the Society's officers as 'Colonel Thompson', the secretary being ever mindful of Thompson's preciseness in these matters and his pride in his war record; but he objected to this mode of address and taking the secretary on one side said 'Rose, to the railway I am Mr Thompson'.

It was company policy during Thompson's time at Stratford to discharge apprentices as soon as they were out of their time. This meant that the newly qualified tradesman had to take his chance in obtaining a job outside the railway, hoping, perhaps, to return in the future. This somewhat Draconian policy dated from the General Strike and its effect on the industry, but it was company policy and no exceptions could be made.

One of the Directors' Scholars finished his apprenticeship but, as he had been a little older than normal in starting his degree course, the end of his indentures and the taking of his final examination did not coincide. This meant that he would be out of a job without having taken his degree and would not be able to support himself during his final year at University. This, of course, must be seen in the context of the times. The 'Directors' Scholars' were unique, University places for apprentices from industry were almost unheard of and anyone aspiring to a University place had to have the financial resources to back it.

The secretary of the Great Eastern Mechanics' Institute, who was somewhat apprehensive of Thompson's autocracy, realised that the apprentice's career might be ruined if he received his notice at such a time, and this would be quite unjust. With great trepidation, the secretary drew Thompson's attention to the anomaly and he promptly tore up the apprentice's dismissal notice, cutting right across red tape and company policy. Thus, the student apprentice went on to complete his course and to spend his working life making valuable contributions to the LNER and later to British Railways.

Thompson was somewhat neurotic about his health and, after an absence from work because of an attack of jaundice, he had thermometers installed in his private office and gave instructions to the effect that the temperature must be maintained between certain limits. On returning from lunch one day, he inspected the thermometers and because the temperature was higher than he had decreed, he seized a cast-iron paperweight from his desk and hurled it through one of the double-glazed windows of his office. He flounced out and snapped instructions to his clerk to have the damage repaired as quickly as possible.

At shop floor level the men rarely came into contact with Thompson - it was almost beneath his dignity to notice them, and any points that had to be raised were usually mentioned to the section head. He would stalk around the works looking to neither left nor right, erect with his chin held high. He had a very quiet speaking voice about which he was very sensitive and had an almost pathological aversion to repeating himself. If asked to do so, even with the most deferential 'Sorry, I didn't quite catch that, sir', he would lose his temper quite irrationally and dismiss from his office the unfortunate questioner, red-faced, into the corridor.

It has been suggested that this over-sensitivity is the reason why Thompson did not present technical papers to the learned societies. He was elected to Membership of the Institution of Mechanical Engineers in 1929 but seems to have taken little part in its proceedings.

The entrance and exit to Stratford works is through a tunnel under the network of lines leading to and from Liverpool Street station. This tunnel connects with Stratford Broadway, and a short distance along the road was a Lyons' café.

Occasionally some of the men from the works would surreptitiously go along to the café and then back to the works suitably refreshed. It was almost inevitable that sooner or later these trips would be discovered, and one morning as three of them were returning, a tall erect figure complete with raincoat and bowler came striding down the road towards them. Their first reaction was to disperse quickly and they headed for the various side streets. Unfortunately, Thompson spotted one of them, but did not, of course, show any signs of recognition.

He sent for the man on returning to his office and the ensuing interview must have been harrowing to say the least. The substance of Thompson's remarks was that he objected to members of his staff running away from him - at least in public. The question of leaving the works for tea or whatever was a secondary consideration - the important thing was appearance.

During the time Thompson was at Stratford he and his wife had a flat in Chilton Court, Baker Street, and as a form of evening relaxation he would stroll along Marylebone High Street to Paddington station. Here he would watch - and listen to – Great Western 'Castles' and 'Kings' leaving with trains for the West and, following one of these excursions, he asked a member of his technical staff, Mr A.E. English, 'What makes the exhaust from Great Western locomotives sound like shots from a gun?' The reply was, 'Sharp valve events with long valve travel, high boiler pressure and a small smoke box, giving resonance'.

Thompson pondered this for some time and then asked what savings could be guaranteed if he converted one of his six-coupled locomotives. Mr English was of the opinion that there would possibly be a 25 per cent reduction in coal consumption.

Amongst the locomotives that had been inherited from the Great Eastern Railway was a stud of 4-6-0s designed by S.D. Holden to handle the heavily-loaded Continental trains from Liverpool Street to Harwich. They were introduced in 1911 and on amalgamation were classified as 'B12s' by the LNER. The maintenance of these locomotives was Thompson's responsibility and by 1932 they were becoming run down. New cylinders were required, some of the blocks being badly cracked and some of the Belpaire-fireboxed boilers were life-expired; thus maintenance costs were high, running costs were increasing, and coal consumption was of the order of 34 lb. per engine mile. Thompson realised that drastic modifications would be necessary if the locomotives were to be turned into economic units and he also realised that he would have to tread very carefully so far as the administration was concerned if he was to rebuild the locomotives in the way in which he thought best.

He requested - and received - authorization for five new cylinder castings and as these incorporated piston valves, new motion was required along with new smokebox saddles.

Thompson then turned his attention to the boilers and pointed out that some of the 'B12s' were ready for re-boilering, suggesting that the standard 2800 round-topped type should replace the Belpaire type. This necessitated a new cab and smokebox and he received the necessary authorization for this project. But far from replacing odd items on odd locomotives, he had used only one of the 'B12s', No. 8579, into which had been incorporated all his ideas. He knew precisely what he was doing and had the foresight and imagination, backed by a team of equally imaginative assistants, to know what the outcome would be. Equally significant is the way in which Thompson manipulated the administration, using all the skill and charm at his command in order to achieve the desired result.

Holden 'B12' class No. 8579 (*centre*) and sister engine No. 8572 receive attention from Stratford shed's engine cleaners.   *British Railways*

During the course of this cloak and dagger rebuild, Thompson paid particular attention to the valve modifications. A full sized mock-up of the valve gear was made and housed in Stratford works and Mr English relates how he spent many afternoons working out the valve events from the mock-up with Thompson enthusiastically turning the handle that operated it.

The converted locomotive was tried extensively on Liverpool Street-Yarmouth turns (known at 'Yarmouth scoops') and the coal consumption dropped quite dramatically from 33.9 lb. to 26.7 lb. per engine mile.

As CME, Gresley was nominally responsible for the rebuild, but the work was carried out entirely under Thompson's supervision at Stratford. It is likely that he proceeded under his own initiative with No. 8579 and in so doing might well have 'hoodwinked' Gresley. The rebuilding of No. 8579 showed judgement and perception and Gresley was apparently satisfied with the outcome, as he authorized the rebuilding of the entire class.

In service, the locomotive proved to be very satisfactory and the rebuilding programme was judged to be successful. Here at last Thompson had produced a series of locomotives with which he would be associated and it came about because the exhaust of Great Western engines sounded, to him at least, like 'shots from a gun'.

Shortly after this he succeeded A.C. Stamer, who retired in 1933, as mechanical engineer for the North Eastern Area based at Darlington. It was a move that pleased Thompson, for apart from the obvious promotion with its increase in responsibility, status and salary, he would be covering the area that was formerly North Eastern Railway territory, an area that held many pleasant associations.

Chapter Five

Darlington 1934-1938

On moving to Darlington, the Thompsons lived for a time in Elton Parade, before moving to Hurworth, a village about five miles outside the town.

Their early months in the North East were saddened by the death in Felixstowe of Sir Vincent Raven in February 1934, but apart from this their domestic life was well organized. Thompson's salary enabled them to live comfortably and to maintain domestic staff to assist with the running of the house. Mrs Thompson's health - always a source of concern and worry - improved sufficiently for her to be able to play golf regularly.

On taking over from Stamer, Thompson assumed responsibility for the Darlington complex which included North Road works, Stooperdale boiler works, Faverdale wagon works - covering some 63 acres - as well as Shildon works, 12 miles away.

His offices were in the former North Eastern Railway headquarters, a massive pile built in the style of a country house, flanked by sweeping drives that led to Brinkburn Road, along which Thompson would walk on his way to North Road works. Mr C.F. Hinds recalls occasions when, on his way home to lunch, the sight of Thompson, erect as always, striding along the road would cause him to double back to the works to pass around the word that the 'Governor' was coming.

Thompson rarely went straight to the manager's office, but would wander round the works before presenting himself.

In 1935, Gresley visited Shildon works accompanied by T.H.W. Cruddas, then smithy foreman at Doncaster. After a thorough inspection of the works, Gresley turned to Cruddas and much to the latter's astonishment asked, 'What do you do, shut it down, or build it up?'

'Tommy' Cruddas, an extremely able man, had arrived in the service of the LNER, via Vickers Armstrong at Newcastle. He had lost his job on Tyneside during the depression and found his way to Doncaster works where he became foreman of the smithy shop. Gresley had heard of his background and ability and, ever eager to make use of people's talents, took him to Shildon works, sought his opinion on the possibility of major reconstruction and received an affirmative reply to his question. As a result of this, Cruddas became resident manager of Shildon under Wells Hood, who had responsibility for both Shildon and Faverdale.

Thompson also thought highly of Cruddas's ability and was solidly behind him in the reconstruction programme. It seems that the two complemented each other: Thompson, Patrician in his manner and academically sound, and Cruddas, with his feet firmly on the shop floor, knowing that things worked but not always fully understanding why they worked. It was this unlikely combination with its energy and drive that was largely responsible for the transformation of Shildon works.

When Wells Hood retired Cruddas succeeded him, remaining in charge of Shildon until his own retirement in 1952.

Elton Parade, showing 'Ferndene', now a nursery. *Jean Earle*

In the years between 1937 and 1947, Shildon works was virtually rebuilt. Of the 10 years that it took, six were under wartime conditions and the following two under conditions of extreme austerity.

Apart from the reconstruction, Thompson encouraged Cruddas to develop welding techniques, particularly in the manufacture of axle boxes and wagon frames. At the same time, wagon sides were being produced by pressing sheets of steel of the correct dimension into U-shaped sections and then welding these sections together to form the body of the wagon. These new techniques enabled wagons to be produced at a much quicker rate than formerly and the knowledge gained as a result was invaluable during the war, due in no small measure to Thompson's foresight.

Another welding attempt that is noteworthy occurred when Thompson tried to have a rocking lever for the Gresley conjugated valve motion fabricated as opposed to forged. The rocking lever was forged in an H-section. The centre pin, situated beneath the smokebox, was a sitting target for ash and extraneous matter which combined with the lubricant to form an efficient grinding compound. The result was wear of the pin and its bearing and subsequent upset of valve events in the middle cylinder.

Old Hall, Hurworth overlooking the river. *Jean Earle*

Gresley seems to have had a blind spot where his conjugated motion was concerned and would not tolerate any criticism of it. It was developed from the designs of H. Holcroft which were in turn based on designs of David Joy, who had used a form of conjugated valve gear on marine engines in the latter part of the 19th century. For full details of the development, the reader is referred to Holcroft's account in his *Locomotive Adventure*.

During Gresley's time when maintenance standards were high, careful attention to the valve gear kept it relatively trouble free. But so far as maintenance is concerned, Thompson inherited conditions far different from those that Gresley had known. Reference has already been made to the heavy demands on locomotives and the shortage of materials and labour. On top of these was the blackout. Maintenance standards deteriorated and troubles with the Gresley derived motion began to show up.

Although Thompson was convinced that each cylinder of a locomotive should have its own independent set of valve year he nevertheless appreciated the fact that the mathematics and the theory of Gresley's conjugated valve year were correct. He attempted to overcome the problem of centrepin wear by reducing inertial forces and fabricating a rocking lever from two half-box sections - placed one on top of the other and welded along the seams. He then proposed to press in a bush for the centrepin. The advantages of this method were that the lever would be lighter that its forged counterpart and therefore not stress the pin as much, at the same time not losing anything in strength, and it would be cheaper to produce. Cruddas was entrusted with the job, assisted by C.F. Rose. Unfortunately, however, it was impossible to check the condition of the weld inside the 'box' and Thompson reluctantly abandoned the idea.

As well as attempting to fabricate the 2:1 lever, Thompson had drawings prepared for the fabrication of the equal motion levers during the time that he was mechanical engineer at Doncaster and in charge of the drawing office. The dates of the various drawings are interesting as they show that Thompson spent a considerable amount of time on the problems associated with the Gresley conjugated motion. The equal motion lever drawings were prepared in September 1940 and approved by Gresley and the 2:1 lever drawings were prepared in 1944.

In 1936, the Thompsons moved from Darlington to the Old Hall, Hurworth-on-Tees. Here they met Maurice and Lilian Hall and began a friendship that was to last until Thompson's death. Maurice H. Hall had, coincidentally, been Sir Vincent Raven's last pupil, but by the time that he met Thompson he had left railway work and was with Firth Brown & Company Limited.

The Old Hall is an early 18th century building with a splendid pediment above the portico and a fanlight reminiscent of that of 10 Downing Street. It seems that Sir Nikolaus Pevsner approved of it - nothing more to add! It changed hands six times between 1890 and 1938 and amongst its occupants were a member of the Pease family, and a Revd William Wrightson who may have been a member of the Head, Wrightson family, Engineers of Thornaby-on-Tees. Also amongst its occupants were the seven batchelor sons of John and Annie Kitching. John's father, Alfred, founded a foundry that subsequently became the Whessoe foundry and he was Mayor of Darlington

Thompson and Tom Hall. The photograph was taken in the summer of 1940.

Mr & Mrs M.H. Hall

1870/71. The seven sons sold the family property to Darlington Corporation and moved into the Old Hall in 1952. Their connection with The Old Hall ended with the death of Herbert in 1965 and the Hall and its contents were sold by auction in 1966.

The Halls' children, Wendy and Tom, took a liking to the Thompsons, who in their turn derived an enormous amount of pleasure from the children's company. There is little doubt that Mrs Thompson's inability to have children was a source of disappointment, but the situation was known and accepted by them at the time of their marriage in 1913.

Thompson always managed to keep his professional life and his home and social life separate. Apart from golf, he had a deep interest in history and geography - he became a Fellow of the Royal Geographical Society - and was an accomplished carpenter.

During the course of a visit to London early in 1937, Thompson was very impressed with the design and lines of a Standard 20 car. The model that he saw was in a West End showroom and had been on display at the 1936 Motor Show. The car, one of only 200 produced, was beautifully finished and was fitted with a V8 engine.

Now, Thompson was never particularly car-minded, although he and his wife had owned various types during their married life, but DLH 1 - the index mark and number of the Standard - appealed to him not only as a means of transport, but also as a fine piece of engineering. Encouraged by Mrs Thompson, he used his powers of persuasion on the salesman, who was at first reluctant to sell the car as it was for demonstration purposes only, and eventually bought it.

The Standard remained in Thompson's possession until shortly after his retirement in 1946, was running until December 1955, and the registration documents were cancelled in 1960.

At this particular period of his life he was settled both at work and at home and in 1937, when Mrs Thompson contracted scarlet fever, he used the enforced quarantine period to write a history of England. His wife was not admitted to hospital and Thompson undertook the responsibility of nursing her, sitting in her bedroom as she recovered, working at his history.

The manuscript of this unique document, consisting of 673 closely-typed foolscap pages, was written primarily for children but Thompson was not interested in having it published which is a pity for it was well-written.

Whilst Gresley was very much occupied with his 'big engine' policy, Thompson was consolidating his position at Darlington. Apart from his personal interest in the re-development of Shildon works, general repairs, conversions and new locomotive construction occupied much of his time. North Road works passed through one of the busiest phases in its history during the four years that Thompson was mechanical engineer. The work for which he was responsible - under Gresley, of course - varied from the reboiling of 'Q5' 0-8-0 locomotives with boilers from ex-Hull & Barnsley 0-8-0s, the rebuilding of Raven 4-6-0s, LNER classification 'B16', and detail modifications of several classes, to the building of a batch of 'V2' 2-6-2s.

Apart from internal work, 'K3s' and 'B17s' were under construction by Armstrong Whitworth and the North British Locomotive Co. respectively and

'D20' class 4-4-0 No. 592 before its rebuilding into a 'D20/2' in October 1942. Unlike its sister engine, No. 2020, she and Nos. 712 and 2101 were to retain their original straight running plate and splashers and cab, although the beading was removed from the rear splasher.   *M.D. England*

'D20' class 4-4-0 No. 2020 as rebuilt in November 1936. Three more locomotives were rebuilt and classified 'D20/2', two in 1942 and one in 1948.

inspectors were seconded to the contractors as quality controllers, the ultimate responsibility for their decisions resting with Thompson. He is on record as stating that the 'B17s' were built because Gresley refused the demand of the Southern Area General Manager for more 'B12s'. Furthermore he stated that the 'B17' was a rush design by the North British Locomotive Co. and that the first batch from North British had the frames removed and replaced with Ducol steel frames within 12 months of entering service.

Some of this activity can be accounted for by a Government-assisted loan scheme which operated in 1936 and 1937 and financed new construction by the company and by outside contractors.

In 1937, Doncaster works was concentrating on the production of 'A4s' and, in consequence, the building of the second batch of 'V2s' was handed to Darlington. Also in 1937, the prototype 'K4' 2-6-0 numbered 3441 and named *Loch Long* was built. This was a three-cylinder machine with 5 ft 2 in. driving wheels designed by Gresley specifically for the West Highland line. Five more were built at North Road in 1938 and 1939.

The year 1938 saw the cancellation of an order for 32 'B17s' which was replaced by an order for 28 'V2s'. This class eventually numbered 184 locomotives, of which 159 were built at Darlington, and is so well known as to require no further comment.

As well as the locomotives already mentioned, 'D49s' and 'J39s' were built during Thompson's time at Darlington, the latter type in varying numbers during each of the four years of his superintendence. The overall effect of the programme was to bring him closer into touch with Gresley's policies and aims than he had been at Stratford. Perhaps one doubtful reminder was the presence of the 4-6-2-2 water tube-boilered high pressure locomotive. This was stored at Darlington from the middle of 1935 until the end of 1936, awaiting a decision as to its future. During its brief life - it was put into traffic in 1930 - it visited Darlington works on many occasions until it made its final journey to Doncaster, whence it emerged in 1937 rebuilt as a conventional three-cylinder locomotive, streamlined but unnamed. Fittingly, the water-tube boiler was installed in Stooperdale boiler shop to provide steam for boiler testing.

Also included in this extensive programme was the rebuilding of a former NER 'R' class 4-4-0 locomotive. This type was introduced by Wilson Worsdell in 1899 and became classified 'D20' on passing into LNER ownership.

In 1936 Gresley modified the design by providing long travel large lap piston valves 10 in. in diameter, altering the splashers and running plate and converting the locomotive to left-hand drive. It was then re-classified 'D20/2', and the remainder of the class became 'D20/1'.

From all accounts it was a successful rebuild and one in which Gresley was very interested. Thompson was responsible for carrying out the work involved, but made the mistake of releasing details to the press without first consulting Gresley. This error might have been an oversight, or it might have been misplaced enthusiasm, but Gresley was not at all pleased and with some asperity left Thompson in no doubt about his feelings on the matter. Unfortunately, Gresley expressed his views to Thompson in the presence of some of the latter's subordinates whilst they were inspecting the locomotive.

Subsequently, three more 'D20/1s' were rebuilt (although not modified externally), but not until Thompson had succeeded Gresley as chief mechanical engineer. Bearing in mind the fact that the 'D20/2' was considered to be a successful locomotive, one wonders why more were not rebuilt - perhaps they revived painful memories!

By the beginning of 1938, Thompson had spent almost 35 years in railway work, the last 15 of them with LNER. His promotions within the company had been progressive, almost predictable, and the announcement in March 1938 that he was to succeed R.A. Thom as mechanical engineer, Doncaster was not altogether unexpected. Thompson was pleased with the appointment and pleased to be succeeding Thom, for whom he had a personal liking, but whom he considered somewhat old fashioned in his approach to railway work.

Mrs Thompson expressed some reluctance at having to move from Hurworth, where her personal life was very settled, but she nevertheless encouraged her husband to take whatever promotion was offered, and as his appointment was effective from 1st July, 1938 she set about the task of setting up home in Doncaster. It was arranged that they would occupy a company house on the outskirts of town, and by the middle of May 1938 Mrs Thompson had decided on curtains, carpets and colour schemes. On 22nd May, after returning to Hurworth from Doncaster, she collapsed whilst watering some plants and died later the same evening.

Thompson turned to and relied on the Halls for support through the difficult days that followed and he moved to Doncaster a month after his wife's funeral. Her personal affairs were put in order - a difficult task, as she had not made a will - and then he had a holiday with Norman Raven in Corsica. Here he immersed himself in Napoleonic history, a subject in which he was profoundly interested, as - significantly - he greatly admired Napoleon.

Robinson 'B3' class 4-6-0 No. 6166 *Earl Haig*, which had been reclassified 'B3/2' on rebuilding with Caprotti valve gear in 1929, seen with with a down excursion train near Northwood in 1938.   *C.R.L. Coles/Rail Archive Stephenson*

Chapter Six

Doncaster 1938-1941

Thompson's arrival at Doncaster was awaited with interest and with curiosity by the staff. His reputation as an aloof autocrat had preceded him and this reputation proved to be correct. He was the antithesis of the ebullient 'Bobby' Thom, who by his very nature had to know all that there was to know and would discuss points at shop floor level in order to keep in touch. His personality filtered right through 'The Plant' and, by contrast, the year between Thompson's arrival at Doncaster and the outbreak of World War II was comparatively peaceful - he seemed to be content to deal with matters of policy, to re-arrange the offices to suit his taste and to delegate details to his works managers.

One of Thompson's tasks at Doncaster was to fit the 'V2s' then under construction with tenders from withdrawn locomotives. This called for modifications, but the net result was a saving of almost 50 tons of steel per locomotive. He also put forward a scheme that involved the rebuilding of former GCR 4-4-0 two-cylinder and 4-6-0 four-cylinder locomotives. The successful rebuild of a former GNR Atlantic 4-4-2 prompted these proposals but the idea was vetoed by Gresley and it was not until Thompson became chief mechanical engineer that he was able to prove his point by the rebuilding of Nos. 6166 *Earl Haig*.

Thompson's ability as an administrator was always acknowledged, and, as his career progressed, this quality became more pronounced. He was punctilious over matters of office routine and if, as a result of meetings with his staff, it was necessary to write letters he would do so before the meeting ended, basing his correspondence on notes that he had taken. He was excellent at dictating and it is recorded that on one occasion he dictated a letter that was three pages long and he did so without making a mistake and without the copy having to be altered.

Thompson now reached what he no doubt took to be his final appointment with the LNER. He was 57 years of age, retirement was only eight years distant, and although Gresley was approaching retiring age he was working as hard as ever and showed no signs of having any intention to retire.

The years immediately before Thompson's move to Doncaster were happy ones not only for him but for the country as a whole. After the upheavals and depressions of the late 1920s and early 1930s, there was a period of comparative stability, with many events to capture the interest and imagination - the Silver Jubilee celebrations, the launching of the *Queen Mary*, the Australian cricketers, and the constitutional crisis that surrounded the abdication of King Edward VIII.

In the railway world, the LNER was on the crest of a wave of prestige that has never since been equalled by any railway company and the pattern of stability was continued during Thompson's first year as mechanical engineer, Doncaster. For him personally life was not easy. Not surprisingly he did not occupy the company house as arranged, but bought a property in St Wilfred's Road, Doncaster. He engaged a housekeeper and began the process of establishing a new routine.

The company, however, went from strength to strength. Under the dynamic and omnipotent leadership of Gresley, these were the Halcyon days - *Mallard* in 1938 and the continued success of the high speed trains in 1938/39.

Although some people were concerned over happenings in continental Europe, the majority was content to reflect on the strength of the Monarchy and the solidarity of the Empire. Gresley's 'A4' building programme was completed and some of the engines, painted Garter Blue, proudly bore the names of our overseas possessions - *Union of South Africa, Commonwealth of Australia, Empire of India* - and no doubt stimulated the jingoist in some of the travelling public.

Following Chamberlain's visit to Europe in 1938, it seemed unthinkable that the social and economic equilibrium should be disturbed, but to some it was obvious that war was inevitable and, in common with other major industries, the LNER prepared itself for whatever the future held.

Under the terms of the Defence of the Realm Act, the Government assumed responsibility for the country's railways and Doncaster was required to tool up for the production of components for tanks and aircraft, the latter being made for the Blackburn Aircraft Company of Brough. This type of work was, of course, new to Thompson and had to be carried out along with routine railway work.

Toward the end of 1940 there was a serious fire in the carriage body shop. At the time that the fire was discovered, German aircraft were passing over Doncaster on their way to bomb Sheffield and although the fire was in no way connected with enemy activity, its cause was not fully determined. Thompson conducted a thorough enquiry into the fire and spent some time experimenting with various materials without arriving at a satisfactory conclusion. The final theory was that the fire started spontaneously in some rubbish in the new workshop adjacent to the carriage body shop, the rubbish consisting of linseed oil-soaked felt offcuts from the weatherproofing material surrounding carriage windows. This was known to be inflammable and there were strict rules about its disposal, but no doubt someone was anxious to get home on Saturday lunchtime and forgot to clear it away.

Damage caused to coaching stock as a result of the fire was estimated at £18,000. More important, perhaps, was the loss of workshop space and equipment. Owing to wartime conditions, the company was unable to start the building of a new carriage body shop until 1947, the work taking two years to complete.

Although the fire had serious repercussions - reorganization was necessary - the war effort and the locomotive building and repair programme had to continue. The two 'lightweight' 2-6-2 'V4s' were under construction, as were a batch of 'O2s' and '8Fs', the latter being built to LMS designs. Gresley gave orders for the withdrawal of the 'A4s' and they were carefully stored at various parts of the system, on the assumption that they would not be required until conditions returned to normal. Doncaster's allocation was four - 4467 *Wild Swan*, 4468 *Mallard*, 4900 *Gannet*, 4903 *Perergrine* (later *Lord Faringdon*) plus the 4-6-4 'W1'. This attempt at preservation did not last very long, however. Demands upon railway capacity increased and the storing of 36 first class locomotives could not be justified. They were returned to service after an absence of only a few months and went on to play a major part in the LNER's vital contribution towards victory.

Chapter Seven

The Years in Office 1941-1946

Every generation needs its heroes and icons and the death of Sir Nigel Gresley following a short illness in April 1941 robbed the railway world of an icon. It also signalled the end of an era and 'the wind of change' blew through the mechanical engineering side of the LNER - it blew more harshly in some places than in others.

There is little doubt that Gresley was on very good terms with his Directors. He had the ability to get the best out of people and he was a brilliant engineer. He had been chief mechanical engineer from the time that the London & North Eastern Railway came into existence and was well liked. In a letter to the author, 'Freddie' Harrison wrote,

> ...of course any great designer can make mistakes and HNG made some good ones! But he never stopped trying out his ideas with the ultimate aim of making the LNER fleet the most successful in the world at that time - which I think he did! [He continues] HNG on the other hand did not dislike Thompson, in fact I don't know anyone that he disliked, he wasn't that kind of person. He thought Thompson was foolish and uncontrollable at times.

And what of the succession? That Thompson was appointed is the *raison d'être* of this book. His competence has been questioned on occasions and it has been hinted that he was unsuited for the job, but consider for a moment the situation facing the Board. Of the possible contenders from within the ranks of the LNER, Thompson, as mechanical engineer at Doncaster, was most senior and had been with the company for the same length of time as had Gresley. Furthermore, he had moved about within the organization to such an extent that he knew every facet of the CME's responsibilities. He had shown himself to be a capable engineer, and he had made positive contributions to the LNER. One correspondent cast doubt on Thompson's ability as an engineer on the grounds that he did not participate in or contribute to engineering discussions. Even if this statement is true, who were the contenders for Gresley's job?

From other railway companies there were few, if any, contenders. O.V.S Bulleid was firmly in command at Eastleigh and received information suggests that approaches were made to him in an attempt to seduce him away from the Southern and back to the LNER. He was, however, fully occupied designing revolutionary locomotives and as he and Thompson had never seen eye to eye, it is unlikely that Bulleid even considered the move.

Overtures were made by the Board of the London & North Eastern Railway to the Board of the London Midland & Scottish Railway with a view to appointing R.C. Bond to succeed Sir Nigel Gresley. At the time, Bond was assistant to W.A. Stanier, then CME of the London Midland & Scottish Railway. Nothing came of the suggestion, however, and Roland Bond eventually held high office with British Railways. The men who in later years also rose to senior positions with British Railways - J.F. Harrison and Robin Riddles come to mind

- were lacking in experience and the fact that the new CME would be following the redoubtable Sir Nigel Gresley would probably be sufficient to deter some aspirants.

On 28th April, 1941,when appointed to the post of CME of the LNER, Edward Thompson could be forgiven for thinking 'Cometh the hour, cometh the man'.

In *British Pacific Locomotives*, C.J. Allen refers to Thompson's succession in Biblical terms. He quotes Exodus chapter one verse eight: 'Now there arose a new King - that knew not Joseph'. This analogy is also used by E.S. Cox in *Locomotive Panorama* and it is this kind of remark that has given rise to some of the controversy that surrounds Edward Thompson.

Shortly after his appointment, Thompson called a meeting of works managers and other senior staff directly responsible to him. As immaculately dressed as ever, he presided in his usual aloof and urbane manner, doing most of the talking. His closing remarks on that occasion were very significant: 'I have a lot to do, gentlemen, and little time in which to do it'.

He took office when World War II was barely two years old, at a time when locomotives were being worked harder than ever before and when reduction in staff and shortage of materials made maintenance difficult. He was 60 years old, fixed in his ways, autocratic, possessed of a sardonic sense of humour, but determined to make his mark. In this he succeeded, but in a way very different from that of his predecessor.

With the change of CME, the Board decided to divide what had been Sir Nigel Gresley's area of responsibility into two distinct parts - mechanical engineering and electrical engineering. Perhaps the Directors felt that it was time that some of the power passed back from the CME to them. Thompson - much to his disgust - did not assume the responsibility that had been vested in Gresley, and the electrical side went to H.W.H. Richards. He - Thompson - showed his resentment in characteristic manner, it was expressed in personal terms, and his relationship with Richards was always very distant.

There was little adverse reaction at Doncaster to the appointment. As mechanical engineer he had his office there since 1938 and in the minds of most people he was the logical successor.

The CME's offices had for some time been at King's Cross, but Thompson decided to stay at Doncaster. Whether or not a distaste for London in the blitz or his settled domestic routine - or both - prompted him to stay at Doncaster, it is difficult to say, but he made his decision and rearranged office accommodation to suit his tastes.

At this time, Thompson appears to have become more autocratic than ever, and he organized and ran his offices with ruthless efficiency. He had the corridor panels in some of his offices reduced in size and panes of glass fitted to the upper portions so that it was possible to walk along the corridor and see into the general offices. He personally supervised the positioning of the office furniture and had the window sills rounded so that they would remain free from 'clutter'. He was invariably the first to arrive in the mornings and the last to depart in the evenings and would periodically inspect his office suite after everyone had gone home. His correctness and attention to detail and his personal standards of dress and behaviour set the tone of his department but

THE YEARS IN OFFICE 1941-1946

were not always conducive to a relaxed working atmosphere. Brown shoes with a blue suit were, to Thompson, anathema.

His attitude towards his staff varied not only according to status but according to gender. He had rigid views on protocol and demanded - and received - the awesome respect that his position with its not inconsiderable salary demanded. Again, quoting Freddie Harrison,

> Once having thought out an idea it was Heaven help anyone who criticised it as being unsound or unworkable, one just had to go along with it until he satisfied himself that it was NDG! But to get him to drop an idea before the damage was done was not only a lengthy but generally a very unpleasant time.

E.S. Cox corroborates this view,

> We were lucky on the LMS in that with Symes, Stanier, Riddles and Ivatt we helots could discuss and contribute. With Thompson and to some extent even with Gresley, Patricians in the mould of bad old Webb, we could only listen and obey or get out.

With male members of staff Thompson could be cuttingly sarcastic and in the event of his having to hand out a reprimand, would do so without regard for the unfortunate recipient's feelings and with the command of English for which he was noted. And yet in his dealings with female members of his staff he was the complete opposite. He is described by one of them as 'charming, pleasant, considerate, and a gentleman', and this particular lady was only a departmental typist in Thompson's Doncaster days.

As was to be expected, there were changes of staff at a senior level and Thompson set about this task as thoroughly as he had set about reorganizing his offices.

A.H. Peppercorn, who was mechanical engineer at Darlington was promoted to the newly created post of assistant chief mechanical engineer. He also became mechanical engineer at Doncaster and in addition assumed responsibility for the York carriage and wagon works and for outdoor carriage and wagon work on the former Great Northern section and on the former Great Central section between Sheffield and London.

In addition there were four more mechanical engineers: at Stratford F.W. Carr; Cowlairs T.E. Heywood - formerly CME of the Great North of Scotland Railway - assisted by K.S. Robertson; Darlington R.A. Smeddle, who also controlled Faverdale, Shildon and Walkergate shops; and Gorton J.F. Harrison.

E. Windle was in overall charge of the drawing office and D.D. Gray replaced T.A. Street as head locomotive draughtsman, the latter being transferred to the Chief Electrical Engineer's Department. D.R. Edge replaced B. Spencer as assistant (technical)

There has been much speculation about the transfer of Bert Spencer and the reasons for it. It is often quoted as an example of Thompson's vindictiveness in that he disliked Spencer for being one of Gresley's right-hand men. I had hoped to have the full and accurate story directly from Mr Spencer, but he died suddenly on 20th July, 1968, three days before I went to Eastern Region Headquarters hoping to obtain his address and to be able to interview him.

Both J.F. Harrison and E.S. Cox were of the opinion that the above assumption is correct. In letters to the author E.S. Cox wrote,

It is a great pity that you were not able to get Spencer's experience, for he was by no means the only one whose career was ruined, not always temporarily as in his case, by what appears no more than spiteful whims.

'Freddie' Harrison,

D.R. Edge's appointment in place of Bert Spencer can only have been an example of ET's vindictiveness. Spencer, on the one hand was a most capable designer with a very sound knowledge of running requirements, whereas Edge, who had been at Stratford with Thompson was basically a carriage and wagon man and not a particularly good one at that: certainly he never filled the position of Tech. Asst. to Thompson as he, Thompson, wanted him to.

E.S. Cox continues,

As you know, there was a time when it was in the balance whether or not I would leave the LMS and go to work for Thompson. If I ever say my prayers, it is to offer one of thankfulness that this never came to pass for there was a darker side to his character that brought terrible injustice to some.

During his time with LNER Thompson had been largely concerned with maintenance, whilst Gresley pursued his ideas and experiments. Under the conditions that prevailed when Thompson took over, it was apparent that maintenance would have to be carried out as efficiently, as expeditiously and as cheaply as possible, these things not necessarily being incompatible. He therefore sought to break down Gresley's 'Ideas Policy', which was a barrier to his interpretation of immediate requirements, by instituting the staff changes outlined above.

On the surface this was a rational and logical move. Thompson was well aware of the nature of the job facing him and he was not the man to tolerate resistance against his aims. It is no doubt the manner in which he brought about the changes - and one can imagine them being carried out swiftly, incisively and autocratically - that caused people to read sinister implications into his actions.

The *Railway Gazette* of 2nd May, 1941 commented on the appointment and included a *précis* of Thompson's background and career.

The *LNER Magazine* of July 1941 summed up the situation:

It will be appreciated that something like a revolution has been made in the methods of conducting the work of the Department, but there is every reason to think that the departures from old established practice will put fresh vigour into the establishment which Sir Nigel had built up since 1923. He left a great example to his successor and the object of all the rearrangements described is to vitalise the mechanical engineering branch of our railway work and so keep the LNER in the forefront as an exponent of modern developments, calculated to secure economy with efficiency.

Thompson followed his staff changes with close examination of the failures of Gresley's locomotives and submitted a detailed report to the Directors for their consideration. He was determined to produce a standard range of locomotives and to follow the LMS policy of building in quantity, using standard components. He disliked Gresley's method of building small numbers of a wide range of types and these factors influenced him in the preparation of his report. E.S. Cox writes,

> In two matters he was quite determined, firstly to do away with the conjugated gear and secondly to use 2 instead of 3 cylinders for all the medium and small sized locomotives. In these trends he was abundantly right but it is a pity that this entirely correct thinking got tangled up with *non sequiturs* like the necessity for equal length of connecting rods.

The first sign, at least to the outside world, of Thompson's maintenance policy - was the removal of the valances from the streamlined locomotives - the 'A4s', the two 'B17s' and the 'W1'. In so doing, he radically altered their appearance, but increased the ease with which they could be maintained. As originally designed, the valances made inspection of the outside motion difficult, although inspection panels were provided, but abnormal working conditions precluded thorough and efficient maintenance - it had to be made as easy as possible. Whether or not Thompson spoilt or improved the appearance of the locomotives is a matter of personal taste. His action was certainly justified as far as maintenance was concerned and it had the added benefit of increasing airflow around the moving parts.

The first of the streamlined locomotives to be altered was 'A4' No. 4462 *Great Snipe*, the alterations being carried out at Haymarket depot under the supervision of T.C.B. Miller. The valancing behind the cylinders was removed completely, but that between the front of the cylinders and the buffer beam was retained and modified so that it could be opened outwards. It was soon realised however, that failure of the fastenings or careless closure of the valance would allow it to swing open and if this happened when the locomotive was running at speed, the results could be disastrous, so the entire valance was removed from all the streamlined locomotives.

The idea of preserving part of the valances was Thompson's and the suggestion was passed to the erecting shop verbally. Incidentally, whilst No. 4462 was undergoing these minor modifications, it was renamed *William Whitelaw*.

Overheating and occasional failure of the inside cylinder big end bearing of locomotives fitted with Gresley's conjugated motion was not unknown and Thompson, who was never an admirer of Gresley's valve gear, was convinced that it was responsible for a high proportion of the failures. He was astute enough, however, to realise that he would have to make out a very convincing case in favour of conversion before the Locomotive Committee would grant the necessary authority, and he invited W.A. Stanier and E.S. Cox to visit Doncaster works to prepare a report on the Gresley conjugated motion.

In the brief section on Edward Thompson in *LNER Steam* (David & Charles 1969), O.S. Nock gives an interesting account of the circumstances leading up to the presentation of the report. He states that Sir Ronald Matthews, Chairman of the LNER, advised Thompson on the latter's appointment as chief mechanical engineer that the designs for new locomotives were not immediately required as the existing stock was quite satisfactory and any additions could be built from existing designs. Mr Nock further related that Sir Ronald was incredulous when Thompson refuted his advice, put forward criticisms of Gresley's designs and went on the ask for an independent assessment, offering to resign should he be proved wrong.

Parts of this account are difficult to accept as, at the time of Thompson's appointment, Sir Ronald had been Chairman for three years and the two had been close friends for almost 30 years. It is unthinkable that the Chairman of the LNER would not be aware of the aims and opinions of one of the company's senior officers on such an important matter as locomotive policy, particularly when that officer had just been appointed to the company's most responsible locomotive post, considerations of friendship notwithstanding.

Easier to accept is Thompson's offer to resign. He was a man of principle and integrity and it is quite in character that if he was not to be allowed to fulfil the requirements of his office as he saw them then he was prepared to go.

Stanier - later Sir William Stanier - was chief mechanical engineer of the London, Midland & Scottish Railway and was greatly admired by Thompson , and it is possible that he thought that by having a report in which Stanier had had a hand, the Directors could be influenced to support the proposed modifications.

The substance of the report was that in a fully run down condition, i.e.: excessive wear in the pins and bearings, losses on the conjugated motion could amount to ⅜ in. This resulted in reduced power at low speeds due to insufficient port opening, whilst the effect at high speeds was over-travel of the valve. This, plus whip in the combining levers could cause the inside cylinder to produce 50 per cent more power than either of the outside cylinders, with the resultant overstressing of the middle big end followed by overheating and in extreme cases complete failure.

'Freddie' Harrison was not altogether convinced and he cited a design fault in the bearing itself,

> ...the straps worked and flexed to such an extent that they could never be kept tight and the subsequent knocking that developed eventually created hot bearings. [He continues] I was well aware of this when I designed the middle big end on the *Duke of Gloucester* which consisted of a very substantial square section strap cottered in position and easily adjustable which gave no trouble whatever.

Thompson followed the report with the fabrication experiments already discussed and the Directors were apparently convinced of the cogency of his arguments, as he embarked upon his rebuilding programme.

Reference has already been made to Thompson's awareness of the requirements of the LNER when he became chief mechanical engineer, and it was clear to him that conditions were unlikely to improve in the foreseeable future. Wartime freight traffic was extremely heavy and there was urgent demand for additional powerful shunting locomotives. There would inevitably be delays in building new ones and Thompson solved the problem in an ingenious way by converting 0-8-0 tender locomotives into tank locomotives. These 0-8-0's - classified as Q4's - had been inherited from the Great Central

Railway at Grouping and were originally designed by J.G. Robinson. Had it not been for World War II, they would probably have been scrapped.

In the course of the conversion, as much material as possible from the old engines was retained, including the cylinders and motion, but the framing at the back end had to be built up to take the tank engine type of buffer beam and draw gear. In addition, the 'new' locomotives were provided with side tanks of 1,500 gallons capacity and bunkers holding 4½ tons of coal. (Some later had 2,000 gallon tanks and 4 tons of coal.)

There were several advantages resulting from the conversion: a supply of tank locomotives, each having its total weight of nearly 70 tons available for adhesion and admirably suited for heavy shunting duties; a saving of an estimated 900 tons of steel, and, as steel castings were not required, demands were not made on foundry capacity. Additionally, the tenders from the original 'Q4s' were allocated to the 2-8-0 traffic locomotives then under construction.

The first representative of the new batch, classified 'Q1' and numbered 5059, was shown to the Directors on 25th June, 1942 - Thompson's 61st birthday - and went into traffic shortly afterwards. A total of 13 was built and proved to be very satisfactory in service.

Dimensions 'Q1'

Cylinders:	dia.	2 x 26 in.
	stroke	19 in.
Valve gear:	outside	Stephenson
	inside	-
Max. cut-off in full gear		75%
Max. valve travel		4⁵⁄₁₆ in.
Steam lap:	outside	1 in.
	inside	-
Piston valve diam.		balanced slide valves
Coupled wheel dia.		4 ft 8 in.
Length of boiler barrel between tube plates		10 ft 2¾ in.
Heating surface:	firebox	141 sq. ft
	tubes & flues	1,068 sq. ft
	superheater	-
	total	1,209 sq. ft
Grate area		23.62 sq. ft
Working pressure		180 lb./sq. in.
Tractive effort (85% boiler pressure)		26.644 lb.
Total adhesive weight		164,976 lb.
Weight of engine in working order		73 tons 13 cwt
Coal capacity		4 tons
Water capacity		2,000 gallons
Brake type		steam and vacuum ejector

Ex-Great Central Railway Robinson 'Q4' class 0-8-0 No. 6132 at Nottingham Victoria *circa* 1926.
T.G Hepburn/Rail Archive Stephenson

Thirteen members of the 'Q4' class were rebuilt by Thompson into 'Q1' class 0-8-0Ts. No. 69936 (originally LNER No. 6179) is seen at Gorton on 4th September, 1948.
John P. Wilson/Rail Archive Stephenson

'J11' Rebuilds

In 1901 J.G. Robinson, CME of the Great Central, introduced his first goods locomotives. It was an 0-6-0 tender engine and the design was a development of the 0-6-0s of Parker and Pollitt. Between the years 1901 and 1910, 174 of these locomotives were built, some at Gorton works and some by outside contractors. As happened on occasions a nickname was bestowed on the class by enginemen and the locomotives were known as 'Pom Poms', on account of their rather sharp exhaust notes. At Grouping, they were absorbed into the LNER and initially classified as 'J11/1' or 'J11/2' according to tender water capacity. Various adjustments were made to the classifications over the years as modifications to the locomotives were introduced. When Thompson succeeded Gresley in 1941, the 174 locomotives were still hard at work.

The 'J11s' were constructed along the robust lines that have always been associated with J.G. Robinson and Gorton works and they were popular with the crews who handled them. Furthermore, they had shown themselves to be capable of a variety of work from slow goods to express passenger and 18 of them had been in service in France during World War I, from which they returned unscathed, apart from one that lost its tender.

In their original form, the 'J11s' were fitted with two inside cylinders, Stephenson's link-motion with slide valves, and Belpaire fireboxes. They were not superheated, but following experiments carried out by Robinson in 1901 on a locomotive fitted with a Schmidt superheater and piston valves, and subsequently with a superheater of his own design, a start was made on equipping all the locomotives with superheaters. It is interesting to note that this work was not completed until 1946.

In view of the proven ability and reliability of the class, Thompson selected it for inclusion and his standardization programme. He intended to re-build some of the locomotives and base a new design for the 'light' goods engine on the rebuilds, and the prototype emerged from Gorton works in July 1942.

The major alterations were made to the cylinders and valve gear and in consequence, the boiler had to be pitched 4 in. higher than in the original and the chimney height had to be reduced to keep within the 13 ft loading gauge. New cylinders were provided, although the original dimensions were retained and the Stephenson valve gear was modified to actuate 8 in. diameter piston valves. These modifications, although far less radical than some of Thompson's rebuilds, necessitated an amount of fabrication work to the frames and were time-consuming. The programme continued slowely as and when heavy repairs became due and by 1946 - the year of Thompson's retirement - 19 of the 'J11s' had been rebuilt and reclassified 'J11/3s', a revival of the classification of the original Robinson piston valve locomotive which had been converted to slide valves in 1928 leaving the 'J11/3' classification vacant.

Eventually, 31 locomotives were rebuilt and as late as 1955 an order was placed for a further eight conversions, but this order was cancelled under British Railways Modernisation Plan.

The Thompson locomotives gave a good account of themselves and on passenger work occasionally reached speeds of 60 miles per hour. They were to

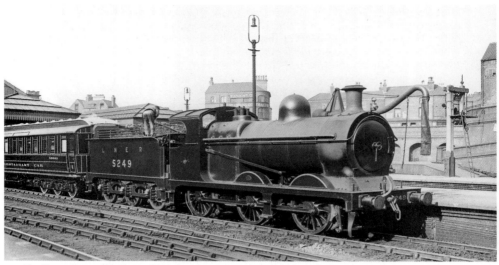

Ex-Great Central Railway 'J11' class 0-6-0 No. 5249 at Nottingham Victoria in1926.
T.G. Hepburn/Rail Archive Stephenson

'J11/3' class 0-6-0 No. 5240 at Nottingham Victoria on 17th August, 1946. This locomotive had been rebuilt from a 'J11' in 1943.   *T.G. Hepburn/Rail Archive Stephenson*

be found at various depots within the former Great Central territory, from Gorton to Neasden, and when the 'J11' class became extinct in October 1962 it was a Thompson 'J11/3' that was the last to be scrapped.

Dimensions 'J11'

		Robinson	*Thompson Re-build*
Cylinders:	dia.	2 x 18½ in.	2 x 18½ in.
	stroke	26 in.	26 in.
Valve gear:	inside	Stephenson with rocking shaft	Stephenson
Max. cut-off in full gear		79%	70%
Max. valve travel		4⁴⁹⁄₆₄ in.	6 in.
Steam lap:	inside	1 in.	1⅝ in.
		Unbalanced side valves	Piston valves 8 in.
Coupled wheel diam.		5 ft 2 in.	5 ft 2 in.
Length of boiler barrel between tube plates		11 ft 4¼ in.	11 ft 4¼ in.
Heating surface:	firebox	130 sq. ft	130 sq. ft
	tubes and flues	1,117 sq. ft	1,117 sq. ft
	superheater	139 sq. ft	139 sq. ft
Total heating surface		1,386 sq. ft	1,386 sq. ft
Grate area		19.2 sq. ft	19.2 sq. ft
Working pressure		180 lb./sq. in.	180 lb./sq. in
Tractive effort (85% boiler pressure)		21,959 lb.	21,959 lb.
Total adhesive weight		116,704 lb.	119,392 lb.
Weight of engine and tender in working order		100 tons 8 cwt	101 tons 12 cwt
Coal capacity		6 tons	6 tons
Water capacity		3,250 or 4,000 galls	3,250 or 4,000 galls
Brake type		steam and vacuum ejector	steam and vacuum ejector

The 'B1'

Writing in the *Railway Gazette* on 15th January, 1943, a correspondent made the following remarks:

That extensive manufacturing resources should be devoted in such a time as the present to the building of locomotives is a striking indication of the importance attached by military and civil authorities to railway transport under wartime conditions. The evidence now is that locomotive building, after having suffered something of a decline is to experience a revival both in this country and in America. A revival of the same kind was recently reported to us to be occurring in enemy-occupied Europe also. In general the engines now being built are of the 'Austerity' or utility type, without refinements, and with many of the parts made by labour and material-saving methods, not hitherto considered suitable for locomotive work. British, American and German varieties of utility engine have already been described in our pages and, elsewhere in the present issue, will be found a description of yet another engine of wartime design. This

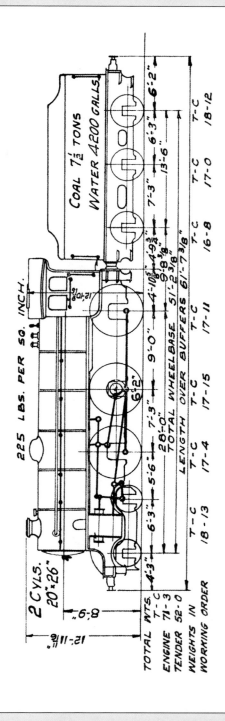

Weight diagram of 'B1' class 4-6-0.

Green-liveried 'B1' class 4-6-0 No. 1225 arrives at Marylebone station with the 'Master Cutler' on 6th October, 1947.   *LNER*

'B1' class No. 1077 in black livery at Nottingham Victoria on 12th April, 1947.

T.G. Hepburn/Rail Archive Stephenson

'B1' class No. 1214 approaches Norton-on-Tees with an express for Newcastle on 6th September, 1947. *W.M. Rogerson/Rail Archive Stephenson*

'B1' class No. 61251 emerges from Elstree tunnel with the 10.15 am St Pancras-Manchester on 9th June, 1948 during the Locomotive Exchanges (*see page 144*). *C.R.L. Coles*

is a new 4-6-0 mixed-traffic tender locomotive recently constructed and placed in service by the London and North Eastern Railway. It is not claimed for this particular design that it is in the 'Austerity' class because, although all reasonable steps have been taken to economise in materials and labour, one of the chief aims kept in view was to produce a utility engine which should be commercially efficient enough to be adopted as a standard type after the War.

These remarks refer to the introduction by the LNER of the first of the 'B1s', a class of locomotive that was destined to become more numerous than any other the company built.

The 'B1s' are generally held to be Edward Thompson's greatest contribution to locomotive design and practice. If it can be said that his star was ever in the ascendant, it reached its zenith in 1942 when No. 8301 later named *Springbok* emerged from the North Road works, Darlington. Here was a locomotive that had about it, at least externally, a suggestion of former days. It was aesthetically pleasing because of its simplicity of line and apart from the raised running plate, did not suggest a departure from tradition.

One of Thompson's early acts on becoming chief mechanical engineer was to cancel an order for ten 2-6-2 tender locomotives, classified as 'V4s', that had been placed by Gresley and were to his designs. Two were already in service and remained substantially unaltered, the only two representatives of the class. The 'V4' was a smaller version of the 'V2' but contained the same Gresley features - 3 cylinders, undivided drive and conjugated valve gear, all of which required careful maintenance and which Thompson disliked.

The cancellation had to be justified and, furthermore, the locomotives had to be replaced by a comparable and acceptable mixed traffic locomotive. And so the 'B1' was conceived out of a desire by Thompson to show that he could design a locomotive equal to the task envisaged for the 'V4', which was basically simpler and easier to maintain.

But did Thompson in fact design a new locomotive? His policy of standardization and ease of maintenance coupled with economy militated against anything new and revolutionary and the 'B1' was a synthesis of designs that had previously been used. By incorporating the best features of existing designs, the expense involved in tooling up for a completely new locomotive was avoided.

The boiler used on the 'B1' was similar to that used on the 'B17', but the pressure was increased from 200 to 225 lb./sq. inch. There was no shortage of steam, as this boiler, intended to supply three cylinders of $17\frac{1}{2}$ in. diameter, was only supplying two cylinders of 20 in. diameter in its 'B1' version, and these cylinders, which were cast from existing patterns, had steam passages modified to give the most direct steam flow that was possible to obtain and drive through Walschaert's valve gear onto the middle coupled wheels.

The construction methods used in the building of the 'B1' showed a departure from the conventional. The greatest possible use was made of fabrication and steel casting was thus kept down to a minimum, only horn frames, wheel centres and buffer sockets having to be cast.

The raised running plate completely cleared the coupled wheels, giving ease of access to the motion, and the locomotive was fitted with a drop gate.

A fine portrait of 'B1' class 4-6-0 No. 61379 *Mayflower* in lined black livery.

Peter Townend Collection

Mayflower's nameplate and a close-up of the steam-driven generator which was fitted to Nos. 61340-61399 from new after problems with alternators on earlier engines.

Peter Townend Collection

The success of the 'B1s' as a class can be judged from the fact that it eventually numbered 410 locomotives, although a number of these were built after Nationalisation, and under British Railways they ranged over the entire system – almost as ubiquitous as Stanier's 'Black Fives' - being amongst the last steam locomotives to be withdrawn from service.

On the 'road' the 'B1' steamed well, as might be expected, and gave a reasonable ride when in good condition. The following log, prepared by the late F.G. Cockman, illustrates the type of performance of which the 'B1s' were capable.

31st March 1960
Train: 3.32 pm Ipswich to Liverpool Street
Locomotive: 'B1' 4-6-0 No. 61373
Load: Tare 305, loaded 325 tons

Miles	Station	Schedule	Actual	Speed
	Ipswich	0.0	0.00	
5.55	Bentley		8.15	61
9.30	Manningtree		11.25	66
12.75	Ardleigh		14.39	63½
17.10	Colchester		18.38	68/47
19.80	Stanway		20.02	51/45
			pws	
22.10	Marks Tey		24.47	53/36
			pws	
26.45	Kelvedon		30.03	71½
			pws	
30.15	Witham		34.02	32
32.85	Hatfield Peverel		38.03	49
39.00	Chelmsford		44.52	71/29
45.15	Ingatestone		51.45	61½
48.60	Shenfield		55.01	65
49.55	Milepost 19¼		55.58	61
50.60	Brentwood		56.56	67
53.85	Harold Wood		59.25	80
55.30	Gidea Park		60.36	74
56.45	Romford		61.36	70
61.45	Ilford		65.56	70
			pws	
62.55	Manor Park		67.16	32
64.80	Stratford		70.47	46
67.55	Bethnal Green Jn		75.31	30
			pws	
68.80	Liverpool Street	83.0	78.10	

pws = speed restriction

The construction of the 'B1s' was unusually slow, the first 10 taking two years to complete, but it must be remembered that war work was in progress at North Road and a balance had to be established between the demands of the LNER and the demands of the Ministry of Aircraft Production, for whom work on the machining of aircraft turrets was undertaken.

At about the same time Thompson reopened the works at Gateshead, originally closed in the 1930s when the plant and machinery were transferred to Darlington.

Thompson was dissatisfied with the availability figures of the locomotives in the North-Eastern area and felt that there was an urgent need to improve upon them, and by introducing selective repairs at Gateshead he intended to increase mileages between general repairs. There is some evidence that Thompson was reluctant to take the above step and there was friction between him and his locomotive running superintendent, Steadman, whom he held responsible for the low availability figures already mentioned. The reopening of Gateshead had, however, two important effects - it kept locomotives at work for an extra 20,000 miles between general repairs, and relieved the pressure on North Road.

Towards the end of the war the availability figures deteriorated and some of the locomotives reported to be out of service had been taken out for trivial reasons. Thompson appreciated the difficulties that were being experienced by some depots –shortages of staff and materials and so on - and he created the post of outdoor assistant to the chief mechanical engineer. Five such appointments were made, one each at Doncaster, Darlington, Stratford, Gorton and Cowlairs. The men appointed worked largely on their initiatives and acted as liaisons between the depots in their respective areas and the Chief Mechanical Engineer's Department.

From then on, some of the problems encountered by the motive power depots were solved and the availability figures improved.

Some of the later 'B1s' were fitted with self-cleaning smoke-boxes. This was basically a wire mesh screen, tailored to fit inside the smokebox and located ahead of the blastpipe. In conjunction with the screen were diaphragm and deflector plates and the object of the arrangement was to ensure that ash that would normally accumulate in the smokebox would be ejected through the chimney. Therefore, there would be a saving of time and manpower, as the smokebox would not have to be laboriously cleaned out by hand. It was discovered, however, that the self-cleaning device tended to restrict draught, and hence steaming, and the best place for the mesh screens was at the back of the shed. Needless to say, this practice was not encouraged.

Although it cannot be denied that the 'B1s' were excellent locomotives, it must be remembered that similar types could perform equally well - the supreme feature of the 'B1s' was in standardization. As noted, their introduction was slow, only 40 being built between 1942 and 1945, but as numbers increased, older types of mixed traffic locomotives were scrapped. In later years, the 'B1s' were not capable of giving the improved services that were required, particularly in East Anglia, and so the 'Britannias' were introduced.

The background to the naming of the 'B1s' is interesting. No. 8301 was widely known as the 'utility engine', and it would not have been surprising had it been named 'Utility', but as its introduction coincided with a wartime visit to this country by General Smuts, then Prime Minister of South Africa, it was named *Springbok* and the locomotives immediately following it were given the names of various species of antelopes. The naming then appears to have become almost casual, but late in 1947, with Nationalisation is sight, it was decided to send some of the 'B1s' into State ownership bearing the names of Directors of the LNER. This was almost a panic move and placed considerable strain on the drawing office, pattern shop and foundry alike - at one stage one pair of plates per day was being cast.

When deciding which locomotive would be graced with the name of a particular Director, it was allocated to a locomotive shedded and working in the area in which the Director lived. For example, No. 1036 *Ralph Assheton* was allocated to the Southern area of the LNER, No. 1189 *Sir William Gray* to the North Eastern area and No. 1242 *Sir Alexander Erskine Hill* to the Scottish area. In all, 18 'B1s' were named after Directors. An air of mystery srrounds No. 1239. It was allocated the name Rupert E. Beckett but it was not used. That Rupert E. Beckett was a Director is beyond doubt as his name appears regularly on the lists of those attending Board meetings. Can we assume that he fell from grace shortly before the naming ceremony or had Rupert E. Beckett no wish to have his name on the smokebox of a 'B1'? That seminal work *Yeadon's Register of LNER Locomotives, Volume Six: Thompson B1 class* - cannot provide the answer and so the mystery remains.The naming of the 'B1s' came as an anti-climax after the graceful and evocative antelope names and, with respect to the Directors concerned, their names were not altogether suitable for adorning locomotives: *A. Harold Bibby*, *Fitzherbert Wright* and *Strang Steel* are but three that come immediately to mind. Still, no worse than attaching *Andrew K. McCosh* and *Walter K. Whigham* to two unfortunate 'A4s'.

Apropos the 'B1s', 'Freddie' Harrison comments, 'On his [Thompson's] own and giving full rein to his natural ability, without being clouded by Gresley phobia, he could and did produce first class locomotives - e.g. the 'B1' and was well able to organize and rationalize the huge department that he controlled'.

Dimensions 'B1'

Cylinders:	dia.	2 x 20 in.
	stroke	26 in.
Valve gear:	outside	Walschaert
	inside	-
Max. cut-off in full gear		75%
Max. valve travel		6⅔
Steam lap:	outside	1⅝ in.
	inside	-
Piston valve dia.		10 in.
Coupled wheel dia.		6 ft 2 in.
Length of boiler barrel between tube plates		13 ft 11 in.
Heating surface:	firebox	168 sq. ft
	tubes and flues	1,500 sq. ft
	superheater	344 sq. ft
Total heating surface		2,020 sq. ft
Grate area		27.9 sq. ft
Working pressure		225 lb./sq. in.
Tractive effort (85% boiler pressure)		26,878 lb.
Total adhesive weight		117,600 lb.
Weight of engine and tender in working order		117 tons 15 cwt
Coal capacity		5½ tons
Water capacity		4,125 galls
Brake type		steam and vacuum ejector

The 'P2' Conversions

Much has been written on the subject of Gresley's 'P2' class of 2-8-2 locomotives, introduced between 1934 and 1936. They were, perhaps, the apotheosis of Gresley's 'Big Engine Policy' - never in this country have passenger locomotives been so massive. The first, numbered 2001 and named *Cock o' the North* made an impact not only on account of its size, but also on account of its appearance. The stovepipe chimney was set on a forward sloping crown plate and the wrapper plates were extended to form smoke deflectors. The second of the class, *Earl Marischal*, was similarly designed but had an extra pair of smoke deflectors fitted.

In 1936, following the extensive testing of No. 2001 at the Vitry-sur-Seine testing plant and close on the heels of the first batch of 'A4' Pacifics, four more 'P2s' left Doncaster works equipped with Bugatti streamlined noses.

A detailed account of design features, teething troubles and performances would be out of place here. In any case, these can be obtained from a variety of sources. Suffice it to say that in January 1943, No. 2005 left Doncaster, not as a 2-8-2 but as a 4-6-2 of hard, rugged appearance, minus its Bugatti nose, and all Heaven was in rage.

Before condemning Thompson out of hand for converting the 'P2s' regarded by many as the desecration of one of Gresley's masterpieces, we must consider the problem facing him. The locomotives as originally built were equipped with the Gresley 2:1 valve gear and undivided drive (apart from No. 2001 which had Lentz rotary puppet valves but was converted to piston valves in 1938), they were prone to hot axle boxes, a fault that emerged at Vitry, rapid wear in journals and connecting rods, which were not helped by the nature of the road over which they were running, and as a result of the size of the locomotives, fractured joints in steampipes was also a recurring fault. They were also reputed to be track spreaders. Perhaps less clearly defined was the human problem of working with locomotives which consumed coal at the rate of 75-90 lb. per mile. This called for an almost superhuman effort from the firemen and it seems fairly clear that the overall running costs of the 'P2s' would be very high. Now if the above is seen against the wartime background and Thompson's preoccupation with maintenance, standardization and availability, the conversions are hardly surprising and were for operational reasons. He is open to criticism for not bringing the entire class to King's Cross and utilising the locomotives on the heavily loaded East Coast main line trains - we read of the wartime feats of the 'A4s' in lifting prodigious loads out of King's Cross and reaching their destination with little loss of time - how much easier would these feats have been to the 'P2s'? It should be remembered, however, that this would have been achieved at the cost of high fuel consumption and Thompson probably felt that the most expeditious way of cutting consumption and turning the locomotives into economic units was to convert them. Anyway, the decision was taken, the Locomotive Committee convinced, and within two years of the appearance of the converted *Thane of Fife*, the remaining 'P2s' had similarly been dealt with.

As stated elsewhere, locomotives' appearances, or at least the rights or wrongs of the appearance of any particular type, is largely a matter of personal taste. To understate the case, the new Pacifics, classified as 'A2s' bore little resemblance at all to the 'P2s'. Reduction of the coupled wheelbase from 19 ft 6 in. to 13 ft, repositioning of the outside cylinders, removal of the streamlined nose and the replacement of the pony truck and leading coupled wheels with a bogie saw to that. The latter, which was one of Thompson's design and which he hoped to standardize, was of the side-support pattern. It took the weight of the mainframe through spherical surfaces onto bronze slippers, the side control being by means of helical springs, and the maximum movement was 4 in. on either side of the engine centre line.

It is worth mentioning here that in introducing this type of bogie, Thompson showed engineering perception. He began replacing Gresley double swing link pony trucks and bogies before accidents occurred (to a 'V2' at Hatfield and the 'W1' at Peterborough).

Coming back to conversions, the monobloc cylinder casting was replaced by separate castings for each of the three cylinders, the bores being reduced to 20 in. and the piston valve diameters enlarged to 10 in. These changes involved the cutting of the front end of the main frame, but as the original locomotives had a spliced front end, the main frame behind the leading coupled wheels was retained unchanged.

As many of the original parts as possible were used, including the outside coupling and connecting rods and motion details. Elimination of the Gresley 2:1 valve gear and the provision of Walschaert's valve gear for the inside cylinder meant that a new inside motion plate was necessary. This formed the main front end support for the boiler and, as it was fabricated, new cast steel frame stays were not required. The drive was divided, the two outside cylinders driving onto the middle coupled wheels and the inside cylinder drove onto the leading pair, requiring the fitting of a new crank axle. It was of the standard form of built-up crank, the web extensions forming balance weights and having an eccentric $4\frac{1}{2}$ in. throw.

By using 10 in. piston valves with longer travel than on the original 'P2s' steam distribution was improved. As there was no change in the lap, wider port openings were achieved from 65 to 75 per cent. Exhaust steam from the outside cylinders passed adjacent to the inside cylinder through pipes taken outside the main frames. These terminated in a single blast pipe to take a Kylchap double blast-pipe and a double chimney, a Gresley feature that Thompson appears to have accepted. As the live-steam passages serving the staggered cylinder layout had to be straightened, the boiler was shortened to 17 in. between the tubeplates.

It appears that at about this time Thompson's attitude mellowed somewhat and he had direct contact with the men engaged on the conversions. He would walk along the half-mile or so of track from his office to the Crimpsall erecting shop, a solitary figure with arms characteristically folded, and check progress with the foreman in charge, Mr 'Billy' Brooks.

Mr Brooks also relates how, towards the end of the 'P2' conversions, he was attempting to locate the cause of a hot box on an 'A4' - a cardinal sin in the book of erecting shop foremen - when he spotted Thompson entering the shop. Thinking that the 'Chief' might want an enquiry into the hot box, and at the same time wishing to ensure that all was going smoothly in other parts of the shop, Mr Brooks did a circular tour and made his way back to the conversions, hoping, perhaps, that Thompson might go away! To his consternation, however, Mr Brooks discovered that Thompson had followed him all the way round, not to have words about the hot box, but to compliment the erection team on the manner in which the conversions had been completed. Shortly after this, Mr L.A. Williamson, who was chargeman erector under Mr Brooks, received the British Empire Medal.

Gresley 'P2' class 2-8-2 No. 2001 *Cock o' the North* in original condition at King's Cross on 1st June, 1934. The rather more conventional steamlined casing shown below on *Mons Meg* was carried by *Cock o' the North* from April 1938.   *Rail Archive Stephenson*

Gresley 'P2' class 2-8-2 No. 2004 *Mons Meg* as built with streamlined casing in July 1936.

No. 60504 *Mons Meg* after rebuilding into 'A2/2' Pacific by Edward Thompson.

'A2/2' class 4-6-2 No. 60506 *Wolf of Badenoch* on Grantham shed on 18th June, 1955.

John P. Wilson/Rail Archive Stephenson

So much for the cause. What of the effects?

In service the locomotives suffered as a result of the reduction of adhesion weight. Coupled with this reduction were boiler pressure of 225 lb., three 20 in. cylinders connected to 6 ft 2 in. driving wheels, the whole giving a high power/weight ratio, the result of being that the locomotives were extremely prone to slipping and were 'light on their feet'. This limited their haulage capacity and their theoretical tractive effort could not be realised in practice. On the other hand, the coal consumption was reduced and the locomotives were more reliable than were the originals.

As well as the obvious operational limitations, the locomotives suffered from prejudice, particularly in the Scottish depots to which they were sent, places in which the name of Gresley was revered and in which Thompson could do no right. By the end of 1949 they were all south of the Border, three at York and three at New England, and were mostly utilised on fast freight trains.

In *British Pacific Locomotives*, C.J. Allen acknowledges the excellence of the front end design of the converted 'P2s' and gives a tabulated log of a run behind No. 60502 *Earl Marischal* (British Railways (BR) number). This shows it to have attained a speed of 95 mph at Raskelf, between Darlington and York, with a gross load of 220 tons behind the tender. Furthermore, Mr Allen states that he believes that this is the highest recorded speed by a British 6 ft 2 in. locomotive on level track.

That would seem to be a fitting note on which to end this section on the 'P2' conversions, but the run referred to was exceptional. No. 2003 *Lord President* (BR No. 60503) took part in trials which will be referred to later, and returned coal consumption figures varying from 70.8 to 45.4 lb. per mile.

Dimensions 'A2/2' and 'P2'

		'A2/2'	'P2'
Cylinders:	dia.	3 x 20 in.	3 x 21 in.
	stroke	26 in.	26 in.
Valve gear:	outside }	Walschaert	see text
	inside }		
Max. cut-off in full gear		75%	
Max. valve travel		6¾ in.	5⅜ in.
Steam lap:	outside	1⅞ in.	
	inside		
Piston valve dia.		10 in.	9 in.
Coupled wheel dia.		6 ft 2 in.	6 ft 2 in.
Length of boiler barrel			
between tube plates		17 ft 0 in.	
Heating surface:	firebox	237 sq. ft	237 sq. ft.
	tubes and flues	2,216 sq. ft	2,247 sq. ft
	superheater	619.67 sq. ft	777 sq. ft
Grate area		50 sq. ft	50 sq. ft
Working pressure		225 lb./sq. in.	220 lb./sq. in.
Tractive effort (85% boiler pressure)		40,318 lb.	43,463 lb.
Total adhesive weight		147,840 lb.	179,340 lb.
Weight of engine and tender			
in working order		161 tons 17 cwt	167 tons 10 cwt
Coal capacity		9 tons	9 tons
Water capacity		5,000 galls	5,000 galls
Brake type		Steam and vacuum ejector	Steam and vacuum ejector

The 'B3/3' and the 'O1'

J.G. Robinson and his design staff at Gorton were never really satisfied with their 4-6-0 locomotives and between 1903 and 1923 produced nine different types culminating in the 'Black Pigs' of 1923.

Amongst this miscellaneous collection of Great Central locomotives that were inherited by the LNER were six locomotives built between 1917 and 1920 and known as 'Lord Faringdons'. They were four-cylinder versions of what were perhaps the most well known 4-6-0 design produced by Robinson - the 'Sir Sam Fays', and like the 'Sir Sams' were dogged by restricted air entry to the ash pan, had an excessive heating surface, were prodigious coal consumers, threw sparks and were poor steamers.

Robinson's experience with the 'Sir Sams' - particularly in the area of maintenance influenced in the choice of four cylinders for the 'Lord Faringdons'. The cylinders were in line, the drive was divided, two sets of valve gear with rocking arms were provided and the locomotives sported various examples of Robinson's fertile mind - 'Intensifore' lubrication system and Robinson superheaters to mention but two.

As an aside, the GCR - and by inference Robinson - was never particularly successful with 4-6-0 locomotives. When the 'Sir Sams' were introduced in 1912, the GCR possessed four classes of 4-6-0 with outside cylinders none of which was covered in glory. Eventually, the 'Sir Sams' were out-performed by the 'Directors' which were two-cylinder 4-4-0s and, according to Dr W.A. Tuplin - never one to heap praise unnecessarily - a 'Director' was one of the most memorable objects in the field of railway engineering.

In 1929 when the 'Lord Faringdons' were being utilised on fast newspaper trains between Marylebone and Manchester and, be it noted, consuming coal at the rate of 96 lb. per engine mile, Gresley had two of them - Nos. 6166 and 6168 -fitted with Caprotti valve gear. He was always keen on trying out new ideas and had approached Caprotti with a view of a conversion, providing that some saving would accrue therefrom. He was assured that there would be a saving in coal consumption, and drawings were prepared and cylinders and valve chests were cast. With 96 lb. per mile to go at, the valve people could hardly go wrong!

The unfortunate part of the conversion was that the maintenance staff was unfamiliar with Carprotti valve year, with the result that valve faces and seatings wore and the coal consumpion gradually increased. No more conversions took place and when No. 6166 Earl Haig now classified as a 'B3/2' fractured its cylinders, Thompson took the opportunity to convert it from four cylinders to two, and equipped it with 10 in. piston valves and cylinders and boiler of the now standard 'B1' pattern.

The rebuilt locomotive was powerful and smooth riding and proved to be quite popular with the crews who worked it, although one unfortunate incident marred its career.

It was fitted with screw-operated reversing gear that after the rebuild worked in the opposite direction to the original. This is something that should have been realised by those directly concerned, but was apparently overlooked. Whilst working a train through Woodhead tunnel, the locomotive stalled and in an attempt to restart it the driver wound the reverser into what he thought was full-

'B3/2' class 4-6-0 No. 6166 *Earl Haig* stands alongside as yet unrebuilt 'B3' No. 6167 at Nottingham Victoria in the 1930s. *T.G. Hepburn/Rail Archive Stephenson*

'B3/3' class 4-6-0 No. 1497 at Nottingham Arkwright Street with the 12.50 pm Nottingham Victoria-Leicester slow on 19th July, 1947. No. 1497 was a rebuilt and renumberd *Earl Haig*, although the engine had its nameplates removed at the time of rebuilding in 1943.
T.G. Hepburn/Rail Archive Stephenson

forward gear. The train ran backwards out of the tunnel and collided with the train immediately behind it, with serious consequences. In fairness to the crew, it must be stated that they would be aware of movement, but in the absence of any illuminated object to which the movement could be related, they would have no idea of direction, short of leaning out of the cab and touching the side of the tunnel. Conditions on the footplate would be far from ideal - an atmosphere that, to say the least, would be polluted and low on oxygen, clouds of smoke and steam filling the cab and the efforts of the crew to restart the train taking place in Cimmerian darkness, pierced only by light from the firebox. It is not difficult to imagine the relief that would be felt when the train eventually moved.

Apart from this, the locomotive performed satisfactorily, and although it remained the sole member of its class, it provided Thompson with the experience that enabled him to re-build a 'B17' three-cylinder 4-6-0 passenger locomotive as a two-cylinder version, classified 'B2'. In a letter to the author, 'Freddie' Harrison wrote, 'All the GC engine conversions were carried out at Gorton under my direction and without doubt [Thompson] improved the GC fleet enormously but apart from the 'O4s' there was no locomotive of any real merit in the fleet. The conversion that I liked best was No. 6166 *Earl Haig* the only 6 ft 8 in. wheel diameter 'B1' - she was a beauty'.

The main dimensions are shown in the table, and the photograph illustrates the appearance of the locomotive, now classified 'B3/3'.

Dimensions 'B3/2' and 'B3/3'

		'B3/2'	'B3/3'
Cylinders:	dia.	4 x 16 in.	2 x 20 in.
	stroke	26 in.	26 in.
Valve gear:	outside	Caprotti	Walschaert
	inside		
Max. cut-off in full gear		65%	75%
Max. valve travel			6⅛ in.
Piston valve diameter		poppet valves	10 in.
Coupled wheel diam.		6 ft 9 in.	6 ft 9 in.
Length of boiler barrel between tube		13 ft 11⅞ in.	13 ft 11⅞ in.
Heating surface:	firebox	163 sq. ft	168 sq. ft
	tubes and flues	1,881 sq. ft	1,508 sq. ft
	superheater	343 sq. ft	344 sq. ft
Total heating surface		2,387 sq. ft	2,020 sq. ft
Grate area		26 sq. ft	27.9 sq. ft
Working pressure		180 lb./sq. ft	225 lb./sq. ft
Tractive effort (85% boiler pressure)		25,145 lb.	24,555 lb.
Total adhesive weight		57 tons 2 cwt	53 tons 7 cwt
Weight of engine and tender in working order		127 tons 10 cwt	119 tons 13 cwt
Coal capacity		6 tons	6 tons
Water capacity		4,000 galls	4,000 galls
Brake type		steam & vacuum ejector	steam & vacuum ejector

Class 'O4/7' 2-8-0 No. 3794 passing through Nottingham Arkwright Street with an up goods on 22nd July, 1947. This locomotive was rebuilt as an 'O4/8' class in May 1957.

T.G. Hepburn/Rail Archive Stephenson

A view of 'O4/8' class 2-8-0 No. 3633 shortly after rebuilding from an 'O4/3' class.

T.G. Hepburn/Rail Archive Stephenson

When considering the provision of a standard heavy freight locomotive, Thompson turned to the ex-Great Central 2-8-0s. At the time, the LNER possessed over 300 2-8-0 locomotives so diverse in detail that there were seven 'sub-classes'.

The basic design of the ex-Great Central 2-8-0 was introduced by J.G. Robinson in 1911, as a development of his 0-8-0 class '8A' locomotive, and gained considerable prestige when adopted by the Ministry of Munitions during World War I for service with the Railway Operating Division in France and elsewhere. They were built in vast numbers by various contractors and in the years following the war most of them were absorbed by the LNER.

There was nothing special about the original design, apart from some typical 'Robinson features' - top feed, superheater header discharge valve, and a smokebox chute intended to facilitate the removal of smokebox 'char'. It seems that these chutes were weaknesses, as they were difficult to keep air-tight, and they were removed in the early days of LNER ownership. From then on, the 'O4s' gained the reputation of being able to keep going and although it would be an exaggeration to say that they throve on neglect, during World War II they ran reliably with low maintenance costs. Along with others, they were described as 'the engines that won the war'.

My introduction to the mysteries of steam locomotive driving came on the footplate of an 'O4' - although to my shame I cannot remember which type it was - on the Worsborough branch line near Barnsley. In company with Gresley's 2-8-8-2 'Garratt', a stud of 'O4s' was kept at Wentworth Junction and used extensively on banking heavy mineral trains up the 1 in 40 gradient to Barnsley Junction. To me, as a small boy, the thrill of an unofficial footplate ride was dampened somewhat by the apparent ease of driving. The engine was buffered up to the guard's van of the train to be assisted, a tug on the whistle cord followed by a few seconds' delay for the response from the pilot engine, the regulator handle was heaved open - a task for which I was once paid a penny- and from then on the engine seemed to manage quite well with the minimum of attention from the driver. The fireman was kept fairly busy during the ascent, but on the return journey he occupied his seat as the engine clanked happily down the bank, waited obediently for the 'road' to be set, crossed over into the siding and then lapsed into simmering somnolence until called upon to repeat the procedure.

As far as I can recall, and I spent many happy hours riding on them, the 'O4s' never failed to respond to the demands of this monotonous existence.

In view of their reputation, diversity and sheer weight of numbers, it is hardly surprising that Thompson decided to use the 'O4s' as the basis for his standard freight locomotive.

He proposed to rebuild them and to reclassify them as 'O1s' when heavy repairs became due, and the first to be dealt with appeared in 1944. The original boiler, with its flat-topped Belpaire firebox was replaced with a standard 100A 'B1' boiler and the two 21 in. x 26 in. cylinders were replaced with cylinders equipped with Walschaert's valve gear. Fortunately, the robust construction of the original locomotive made the accommodation of the new parts possible without the frames having to be strengthened and, as will be seen from the accompanying table, there was little difference in weight between 'O4' and 'O1'.

The *Railway Gazette* of 1st September, 1944 carried a brief account of the conversion and commented on the change in the appearance of the locomotive – 'it

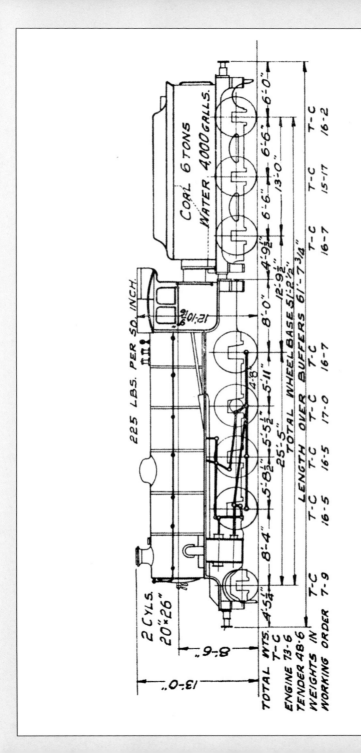

Weight diagram of 'O1' class 2-8-0.

now has all the looks of a Doncaster locomotive' - and a week later published a letter under the pen-name 'Scrutator' that made the following point: 'Isn't it [sic] time, however, that the LNER dropped the use of the word "conversion" in respect of the large-scale locomotive changes? Mr E. Thompson, the Chief Mechanical Engineer, is really building new engines, but is using the sound parts of old locomotives as, indeed, has been done often enough with all rolling stock. If Mr J.G. Robinson had been in the land of the living, he could hardly have found fault with the appearance of the new engine, which has replaced that which he designed.'

The reconstruction of the 'O4s' was extensive, time-consuming and expensive, but the costs were more that offset by the economies that resulted.

The 'O1' was a much better all-round machine than the 'O4'. Tractive effort was increased by almost 13 per cent, and the power classification was raised from '7F' to '8F'. The locomotive enabled the Annesley-Woodford coal trains to be operated 'out and home' on a regular pattern and this brought about great savings in the service.

The rebuilding programme went ahead steadily and was continued by Thompson's successor. By the time that the introduction of British Railways' standard types put an end to it, 58 'O4s' had become 'O1s'.

The 'O1' was a useful locomotive and undoubtedly justified its rebuilding and modernisation. It was a pity that Thompson retained the original axle boxes, as these were prone to run hot, but, apart from this, he achieved a standard locomotive at a cost considerably lower than that of scrapping the 'O4s' and constructing the new 'O1s'.

Dimensions 'O4' and 'O1'

		'O4'	'O1'
Cylinders:	dia.	2 x 21 in.	2 x 20 in.
	stroke	26 in.	26 in.
Valve gear:	outside	Stephenson	Walschaert
	inside		
Max. cut-off in full gear			75%
Max. valve travel			$6^{21}/_{32}$ in.
Steam lap:	outside		
	inside		$1\frac{5}{8}$
Piston valve dia.		Slide valves	10 in.
Coupled wheel dia.		4 ft 8 in.	4 ft 8 in.
Length of boiler barrel between tube plates		15 ft	13 ft $11\frac{7}{8}$ in.
Heating surface:	firebox	154 sq. ft	168 sq. ft
	tubes and flues	1,349 sq. ft	1,508 sq. ft
	superheater	242 sq. ft	344 sq. ft
Total heating surface		1,745 sq. ft	2,020 sq. ft
Grate area		26.24 sq. ft	27.9 sq. ft
Working pressure		180 lb./sq. in.	225 lb./sq. in.
Tractive effort (85% boiler pressure)		31,326 lb.	35,518 lb.
Total adhesive weight			147,504 lb.
Weight of engine and tender in working order		73 tons 4 cwt (engine only)	121 tons 12 cwt
Coal capacity		6 tons	6 tons
Water capacity		4,000 galls	4,000 galls
Brake type		Steam	Steam

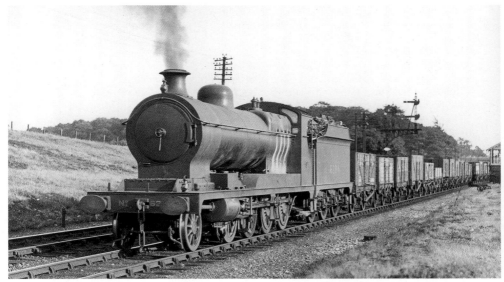

'O4' class No. 6284 with a down goods on the Great Northern main line passing Greenwood signal box in 1925.   *F.R. Hebron/Rail Archive Stephenson*

Fifty-eight members of the 'O4' class were rebuilt to become Thompson's 'O1' class 2-8-0s. No. 3687 passes Nottingham Victoria with an up goods train on 19th April, 1947. This engine was rebuilt from 'O4' class No. 6324 to an 'O1' class in December 1945.

T.G. Hepburn/Rail Archive Stephenson

The A2/1's

Thompson was satisfied with the success of the 'P2' conversions to the extent of ordering the last four of a batch of 25 2-6-2 mixed traffic locomotives to be built as Pacifics. These 2-6-2s were Gresley's famous 'Green Arrows', the 'V2s'. Constructed between 1936 and 1944 and eventually totalling 184 locomotives, the class won high praise for its ability to handle express freight and express passenger with equal facility - it was very much the LNER's 'maid of all work' class.

The decision to turn out the last of the class as 4-6-2s was based upon the familiar maintenance and standardization argument and it was another step towards the creation of a class of Pacifics intended to take over the role of the 'A4s'.

Thompson has now been chief mechanical engineer for three years and was pursuing his policies with as much zeal and determination as ever. He seems to have established a satisfactory working relationship with the Locomotive Committee, which was under the chairmanship of Andrew K. McCosh, a formidable Scotsman, frank and forthright, calling a spade very much a spade. As a Director, he had clashed with Gresley until the pair of them decided that co-operation was better for all concerned, and the company in particular, than antagonism.

Apart from support from the Locomotive Committee, Thompson had a staunch ally in the Chairman of the company, Sir Ronald Matthews, and this friendship might well have influenced the Committee in its decisions.

Always a hard and tireless worker, Thompson continued with apparently boundless energy. He expected the same attitude from this subordinates, but he did not expect their efforts to go unrewarded and he was careful to keep a check on wages and salaries and to ensure that everyone under his control was paid 'the rate for the job'. There are instances of staff at all levels having unexpected rises, usually at Thompson's instigation.

With the pressures of work being so great, Thompson had little time - or inclination - for social activities. Always aloof, he resisted attempts that were made to involve him in various organizations and was content to spend his leisure time at home. His main relaxation, apart from golf, were the weekends that he spent with the Halls at Brymbo. He went as often as possible, usually every third weekend, leaving Doncaster on Friday afternoon and returning on Monday morning.

During the weekends that he stayed in Doncaster, he invariably worked on Sunday mornings, and would occasionally visit Sir Ronald and Lady Matthews either at their home in Sheffield or at their weekend cottage near Newark. Thompson was on extremely good terms with the Matthews's, Lady Matthews being a frequent visitor to his office, and she took a keen interest in his work.

The de-greasing and cleaning of locomotive frames in 'The Plant' was a laborious and filthy business and during the war was carried out by female employees. It involved the mixing of a degreasing substance with sawdust, applying the mixture to the frames and then scraping it off. On seeing a group of women engaged on the task, Lady Matthews was horrified and asked

'A2/1' class 4-6-2 No. 3698 fitted with electric lighting and a Metro-Vickers axle-driven generator. Lamp brackets had to be fitted for daylight use, although hinged discs were tried on this locomotive for a time but were prone to damage.   *LNER*

whether or not the mixture could be hosed from the frames? This method had not occurred to Thompson, but he acted promptly on the suggestion and, in due course, pumps and hoses arrived from Stratford and the lot of the degreasing gang was eased, thanks to Lady Matthews' interest.

Although the demands on Thompson's time were legion - he was away from Doncaster for perhaps an average of two days a week, hence the necessity to work on Sunday mornings - he managed to have some holidays. He was very fond of the Tregenna Hotel at St Ives and spent some of his wartime holidays there, and on one occasion managed a golfing holiday at St Andrews with his brother-in-law, Norman Raven. These periods of recreation were, however, taken at lengthy intervals and were quite short. Thompson was far too wrapped up in his work to spend too long away from it, and in this he was unwise, but due allowance must be made for the man, the job and the times.

Thompson made a point of visiting the works under his control as often as possible and he had to divide his time between meetings of the Locomotive Committee, CME's meetings, meetings with Sir Alan Mount, HM Inspector of Railways (for whom Thompson had scant regard and referred to as 'Sally' Mount), all these taking place at regular intervals and, of course, the routine in his office.

He would, for instance, visit Darlington about once a month, usually giving notice of his proposed visit. This was viewed with slight misgivings as Thompson was somewhat unpredictable. A chance remark might give him obvious pleasure, but it might cause him to lose his temper. It was never quite certain which way he would react, but after the remark had been made it was too late to do much about it.

He was at various times at odds with all of his immediate subordinates, and as someone remarked about Thompson when we was in one of his irascible moods, 'he considered everyone to be a bloody fool'.

As might be expected, he faced the prospect of retirement with some apprehension. He prepared for it to the extent of buying a house in Westgate and had alterations to it carried out, but his attitude is aptly illustrated by a comment that he made to his secretary on a grey, wet day. Looking out of his office window across the rain-soaked 'plant' he said, 'What does one do on a day such as this when one is retired?'

Shortly after this, Thompson's house was damaged by bombing, so he moved some of his personal possessions into his office, including 35 suits! He also had a bed in his office and used to take his turn on fire watching duty.

He made arrangements to have his Standard 20 laid up for the duration of the war and replaced it with a Fiat 500. Squeezing in and out of it was quite a performance for Thompson - he was over 6 feet tall - and he ran the car until the Italians entered the war when he patriotically sold it and took to cycling or to using company transport.

The first of the four Pacific locomotives that replaced the last four 'V2s' left Darlington works in March 1944. Classified 'A2/1', it was very similar in appearance to the modified 'P2' but it was provided with a six-wheeled tender.

A bogie identical with that used on the 'B1s' replaced the original pony truck and the whole of the bogie stays and spring bracket were of welded

An official broadside portrait of 'A2/1' class 4-6-2 No. 3696.   *LNER*

The cab layout of 'A2/1' class No. 3698 showing the electrically illuminated gauges and the Great Central-type regulator handle.   *National Railway Museum*

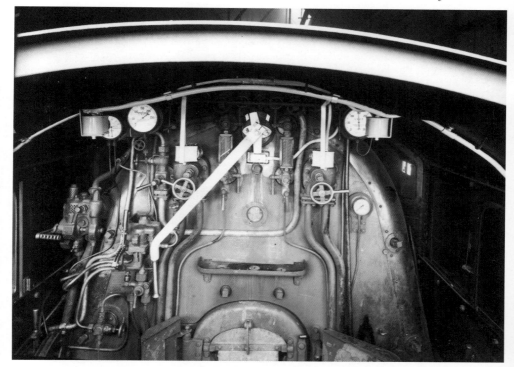

construction, as were the front end boiler support stay, quadrant link brackets and footplate brackets.

The three cylinders were equipped with independent sets of valve gear, thus eliminating the Gresley 2 :1 valve gear for the inside cylinder, as on the 'V2s', and the drive was divided between the leading and middle coupled axles, with connecting rods of equal length. This meant that the staggered cylinder layout used in the 'P2' rebuild had to be retained and consequently, the cylinders were cast separately. Comment has been passed on Thompson's use of separate castings instead of a one-piece or monobloc casting for three cylinders. In order to accommodate divided drive and identical length connecting rods, it was necessary to stagger the cylinder layout and a monobloc casting to this design would have been difficult and expensive to produce.

Thompson's near fixation with equal length connecting rods was based upon his experience at Stratford. Frothing of the lubricant of an inside cylinder big end had been giving some trouble and this was eventually traced to unequal stresses in the bearing created in an error in the ratio of the horizontal distance moved by the connecting rod of the vertical distance by the big end.

The monobloc cylinder casting was introduced by Vincent Raven on his 'Z' class North Eastern Railway 'Atlantic' and subsequently used for all his three-cylinder designs. Gresley also used monobloc castings on several of his designs and, whilst they were generally trouble free, the major disadvantage was that if one cylinder was damaged or broken, all three had to be removed. Under conditions of shortage of materials and demands on machine shop capacity it was logical that Thompson should revert to single castings. In so doing, however, he created maintenance problems as the cylinders of his Pacifics worked loose and this was not an easy fault to rectify.

As many components as possible from the 'V2' 2-6-2s were used in the 'A2/1s'. The type 109 boiler and firebox was retained but with the working pressure increased by 5 lb. per sq. in to 225 lb. per sq. in. The cylinder diameter was increased by ½ in. and the cut-off from 65 to 75 per cent. The overall effect of these alterations was to increase the tractive effort by approximately 8 per cent.

As the construction of the prototype was nearing completion, Thompson paid one of his periodic visits to North Road works. Accompanied by R.A. Smeddle, mechanical engineer, Darlington and C.G. Gould, works manager, he inspected the locomotive and announced his intention of fitting it with identification discs. (This was not a new idea, as discs had been used by other companies and indeed other sections of the LNER for some years. It must be remembered that the purpose of lamps on locomotives was purely for identification for the convenience of the operating people and that white discs could do the job just as effectively, particularly in daylight.)

He complained bitterly about the way in which locomotives head and tail lamps were treated and argued that crews were careless with them, and from an economic point, money was being wasted.

All was well until Mr Gould pointed out that a disc fitted in the conventional lamp bracket position at the top of the smoke box door would foul the loading gauge whereupon Thompson, much to Mr Smeddle's alarm became quite irate.

'A2/1' class No. 508 *Duke of Rothesay* emerges from Welwyn North tunnel with a King's Cross-Peterborough North slow train in 1947.   *F.R. Hebron/Rail Archive Stephenson*

'A2/1' class No. 60510 *Robert the Bruce* in British Railways days.   *Peter Townend Collection*

He immediately ordered a ladder to be brought, set it against the smokebox door and mounted it, insisting that Mr Gould accompanied him, which he did, to a muttered aside, 'You got yourself into this. Now get out of it.' On examination, however, Thompson agreed that Mr Gould had a point and calmed down.

After alterations to the fittings, the locomotive was equipped with discs and worked between Darlington, Harrogate and Leeds on running-in-turns. The LMS operating authorities were notified, as it had to travel over their lines before entering Leeds City station, but in spite of the preparations, the identification disc idea was not perpetuated and No. 3696 was the only member of its class fitted with them. Why this was so is not clear. It was unlike Thompson to allow the matter to be quietly dropped, but at this particular time he was under great pressure and it can only be assumed that no one troubled to remind him.

The four locomotives were eventually given names in keeping with those of the 'A2/2s' and after moving around the system, three of them (BR Nos. 60507/9/10) went to Haymarket Depot, Edinburgh, whilst No. 60508 was stationed at New England. It was this locomotive that was involved in the New Southgate accident in July 1948.

The class underwent minor modifications during its working life, including the renewal of the steam-operated reversing gear, replacement of the swing type regulator handle with a Gresley pull-out type and, perhaps a most noticeable change, the provision of eight-wheel tenders, one of these coming from 'A4' Pacific *Sir Ralph Wedgwood*. This engine was damaged beyond repair during an air raid in 1942. The six-wheeled tenders displaced by the changeover were allocated to 'B1s'.

The Haymarket engines worked reliably and well, but No. 60508 seems to have passed it days fairly quietly. There are no records of any of them having produced outstanding performances and the class was withdrawn between August 1960 and March 1961.

As with the converted 'P2s', erroneous conclusions have been drawn about the scrappings. In both cases, rapid dieselisation was responsible for the locomotives being withdrawn from service earlier that would have been normal. The member of Headquarters staff responsible for the withdrawal programme had a tidy mind and picked smaller classes and odd locomotives for scrapping before the numerically larger classes. In this he was quite justified and so the early demise of the Thompson 'A2/1' and 'A2/2' classes suited the statisticians. It also suited his critics, but once again, the facts prove them to be wrong.

After the conversion of the 'P2s' to 'A2/2s' and the reconstruction of the 'V2s' to 'A2/1s', Thompson had nine Pacific locomotives with many details in common, and conforming to his overall plan. He had incorporated features that he thought were important, such as rocking grates, hopper ashpans and valve gear that required the minimum of attention. He had also been able to use and to develop up-to-date techniques in construction and his programme had continued alongside the essential Government work that was being carried out in the company's workshops.

'B16' class 4-6-0 No. 2381 approaches Scarborough with an excursion train from Bradford in June 1925.   *F.R. Hebron/Rail Archive Stephenson*

'B16/3' class 4-6-0 No. 922 at Nottingham Victoria with a train of Woodford Halse-Annesley coal empties on 3rd July, 1946. This locomotive had been rebuilt from a 'B16' class in April 1944.
                                                                                                      T.G. Hepburn/Rail Archive Stephenson

The locomotives were tried under varying conditions of express passenger work and the experience gained provided Thompson with information that enabled him to take another step towards his 6 ft 8 in. coupled wheel Pacific.

Dimensions 'V2' and 'A2/1'

		'V2'	'A2/1'
Cylinders:	dia.	3 x 18½ in.	3 x 19 in.
	stroke	26 in.	26 in.
Valve gear:	outside	Walschaert	Walschaert
	inside	Gresley	Walschaert
Max. cut-off in full gear		65%	75%
Max. valve travel		5⅜ in.	6¼ in.
Steam lap:	outside	1⅝ in.	1⅝ in.
	inside	1¹¹⁄₁₆ in.	1⅝ in.
Piston valve dia.		9 in.	10 in.
Coupled wheel dia.		6 ft 2 in.	6 ft 2 in.
Length of boiler barrel between tube plates		17 ft 0 in.	16 ft 11⅝ in.
Heating surface:	firebox	215 sq. ft	215 sq. ft
	tubes and flues	2,216.07 sq. ft	2,216.07 sq. ft
	superheater	679.67 sq. ft	679.67 sq. ft
Total heating surface		3110.74 sq. ft	3110.74 sq. ft
Grate area		41.25 sq. ft	41.25 sq. ft
Working pressure		220 lb./sq. in	225 lb./sq. in.
Tractive effort (85% boiler pressure)		33,730 lb.	36,387 lb.
Total adhesive weight		146,944 lb.	147,840 lb.
Weight of engine and tender in working order		145 tons 2 cwt	158 tons 7 cwt
Coal capacity		7½ tons	9 tons
Water capacity		4,200 galls	5,000 galls
Brake type		Vacuum	Steam and vacuum ejector

The 'B16/3'

The former North Eastern Railway class 'S3' 4-6-0 locomotive was introduced by Sir Vincent Raven in 1919 and was designed to provide an increase in power for mixed traffic work over his 'S2' 4-6-0s.

Opinions differ over the success of the 'S3' - it was described to me in one interview as 'wretched' and in another as 'thoroughly successful'. The engines were three-cylindered with three sets of Stephenson link motion operating the piston valves, the motion being situated between the frames. There was a monobloc casting for the cylinders and the drive was taken through short connecting rods to the leading pair of coupled wheels.

The positioning of the valve gear made inspection and maintenance difficult and a driver had to be something of a contortionist in order to squeeze around the running gear to inspect and lubricate it - there were six eccentrics and a big end between the frames.

Another unhappy feature was the steam-operated reversing gear with which the locomotives were fitted. Variations in steam pressure in the reverser slave cylinders could make adjusting the cut-off something of a hit or miss business and would occasionally allow a locomotive to go into full forward gear whilst running at speed. This had the disconcerting effect of taking the fire out through the chimney and if, as happened once, the locomotive was passing through a station, parts of the station roof disappeared with the fire.

Building of the 'S3s' continued until 1924 and the class eventually numbered 70 locomotives, which were designated 'B16s' under the LNER classification.

In 1937 Sir Nigel Gresley rebuilt one of the 'B16s' - No. 2364 - fitted with new cylinders, the outside pair having Walschaert's valve gear and the inside one having Gresley's conjugated motion with rocking arms behind the cylinder. Alterations were made to the framing and footplating, but the boiler was retained with the pressure unaltered. The rebuilding was carried out at Darlington works under Thompson's direction and between 1937 and 1940 seven engines were similarly rebuilt and classified 'B16/2'.

As part of his standardization plans, Thompson decided to retain the 'B16s' as mixed traffic 4-6-0s, a decision that Mr O.S. Nock in his *Locomotives of the LNER* describes as 'interesting'. In view of some of the problems associated with the class the decision was indeed interesting, but it was a numerically large class and its members were not old by railway standards. By introducing a rebuilding programme, Thompson would provide the LNER with a stud of 4-6-0 locomotives capable of a wide range of duties, with the minimum of expenditure. As has already been noted, Thompson was quick to use existing classes of locomotives for rebuilding if he considered that they had potential, as instanced by the use of some of the former Great Central engines to contribute to his programme.

The first Thompson rebuilt 'B16' left Darlington in May 1944 and, between then and 1947, 17 were converted and classified 'B16/3'. They were equipped with three separate sets of Walschaert's valve gear which, by its design was far more accessible that the Stephenson link motion that it replaced. New cylinder castings were provided, but the dimensions were unchanged, as was the boiler pressure and, consequently, the tractive effort was not altered.

The 'B16s' were successful from their introduction. They were popular with crews, were economical and had good riding qualities. Unfortunately, the rebuilding programme did not continue for very long after Thompson's retirement and it is rather ironic that this attempt to standardize was discontinued as the result of other standardization plans - those proposed under British Railways. This decision left the former LNER with three different types of 'B16'.

Although the original 'B16s' could be troublesome, they were capable of good performances. In *Four Thousand Miles on the Footplate* Mr O.S. Nock records that one of them - No. 61426 - hauled 43 unbraked wagons, a gross load of 750 tons, between York and Mexborough and reached a speed of 34½ mph at Ackworth.

Dimensions 'B16/3'

Cylinders:	dia.	3 x 18½ in.
	stroke	26 in.
Valve gear:	outside	Walschaert
	inside	Walschaert
Max. cut-off in full gear		75%
Max. valve travel		6⅜ in.
Steam lap:	outside	1⅝ in.
	inside	
Piston valve dia.		9 in.
Coupled wheel dia.		5 ft 8 in.
Length of boiler barrel		
between tube plates		
Heating surface:	firebox	169.4 sq. ft
	tubes and flues	1,811.5 sq. ft
	superheater	446.4 sq. ft
Total heating surface		2,427.3 sq. ft
Grate area		23.7 sq. ft
Working pressure		180 lb./sq. in
Tractive effort (85% boiler pressure)		30,031 lb.
Total adhesive weight		131,488 lb.
Weight of engine and		
tender in working order		125 tons 11 cwt
Coal capacity		5½ tons
Water capacity		4,125 galls
Brake type		Steam and vacuum ejector

The 'L1'

The first completely new locomotive design to be introduced after the war by any of the four railway companies was Thompson's 2-6-4 tank engine. It was intended to meet the demands for a tank engine with sufficient water capacity to enable it to undertake duties on which it had been necessary to use tender engines, at the same time keeping within the axle loading limits, as well as to provide a general utility locomotive of high power and acceleration for conventional tank engine duties.

Classified as 'L1', the prototype locomotive, No. 9000, was turned out of Doncaster works resplendent in apple green livery and underwent trials on a wide variety of passenger duties, including main line express working between Leeds and Doncaster. It had two outside cylinders, 20 in. diameter, 26 in. stroke, similar to those used on the 'B1' 4-6-0s and a 'V3' type boiler, the working pressure of which was raised from 220 to 225 lb. per sq. in., and with a larger firebox. The coupled wheels were of 5 ft 2 in. diameter, smaller than was customary for a passenger train, but it was thought that they would be big enough for the maximum speed that was likely to be required, at the same time ensuring rapid starting and acceleration, a vital feature for surburban working. The small wheels would also make the engine adaptable for universal train work.

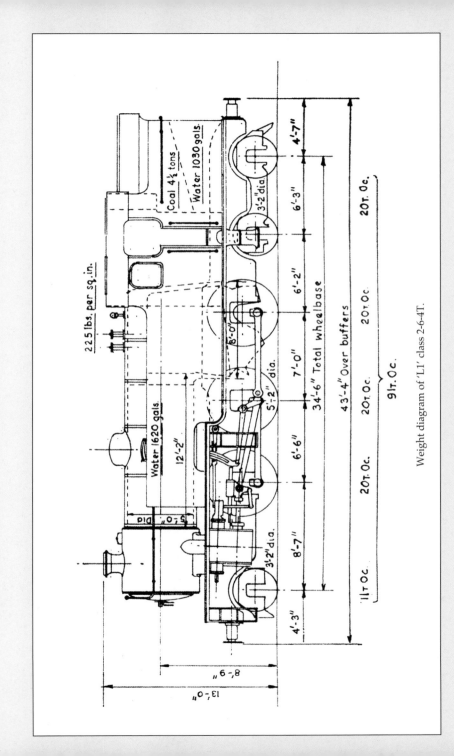

Weight diagram of 'L1' class 2-6-4T.

The tanks and bunker were of high capacity and of welded construction, holding 2,630 gallons of water and 4½ tons of coal respectively.

The comfort and convenience of the crew were taken into consideration, for as well as the fitting of electric lights in the cab, and the illumination of the main gauges, the view when running bunker first was excellent, a feature that was far from ideal in other designs.

In order to conform with the operational requirements of the Eastern Section of the LNER, Westinghouse brakes were fitted along with a vacuum ejector.

In the trials already mentioned, the 'L1' was worked against various locomotive types ranging from ex-GER 2-4-2 and LNER 2-6-2 tank engines to the 'B12/2' and 'B1' 4-6-0 tender engines. On one particular occasion, it worked a 366 ton express train from Liverpool Street to Ipswich at a water consumption rate of less than 30 gallons per mile and completed the round trip, with a return load of 386 tons, at an average coal consumption of 0.093 lb. per train ton mile. This performance must, however, be regarded as exceptional, as the locomotive was designed to be a general utility short distance type that could be used with equal facility on passenger and goods work. No. 9000 was also tried on coal trains, but was not successful. Although the class was designed with short haul colliery work in mind - the high tractive effort is indicative of this - it is thought that insufficient braking capacity and lack of adhesion militated against it.

The thread of Thompson's policy can be seen running through the design - standard parts, standard construction techniques, high availability, and as will be noticed from the photographs, the stepped running plate gave easy access to the motion, hence ease of maintenance.

In service, however, the picture was very different.

Although the prototype had acquitted itself well, the class as a whole did not come up to its designer's expectations. Ironically, the 'L1s' were troublesome to operate and expensive to maintain. After the fitting of self-cleaning smoke boxes without any improved draughting became standard practice they were temperamental steamers and unless they were handled very carefully by crews who were prepared to understand and 'nurse' them, they were quite unreliable. Some of the King's Cross batch of 'L1s' were allocated to Hitchin and in, the hands of regular crews, ran quite well, but it was a different story when an 'L1' was allocated as an odd turn to a King's Cross crew. They, of course, were used to Pacifics and 'V2s' and very quickly discovered that their normal handling techniques could not be applied to the 'L1s'. It was in fact necessary to send an inspector with a crew unused to the ways of the 2-6-4Ts when working them for the first time. As Mr C.N. Morris, formerly divisional maintenance engineer at King's Cross put it, 'You did not as such drive an 'L1' as scheme it along'. Some of the 'L1s' were used on empty stock working at King's Cross, and had great difficulty in moving heavy sleeping car trains through tunnels. Slipping became such a problem that there was almost daily disruption to services whilst the line was cleared. Eventually double heading was resorted to, but bad weather, bad rail conditions, and low adhesive factor emphasised the difficulties.

Another recurring source of trouble was the bearing surfaces of the axle boxes. They could not stand the loads imposed on them and wore very rapidly due in no small measure to the locomotives being over-cylindered. This

'L1' class 2-6-4T No. 9000 at Stratford in 1945. It was the only member of the class built prior to nationalization and the formation of British Railways.   *Photomatic/Rail Archive Stephenson*

'L1' class No. E9005 at Doncaster on 20th March, 1948. This locomotive had entered service the previous month. The LNER-allocated number of 9005 carries a prefix, 'E', which denotes British Railways Eastern Region. The first 39 'L1s' to be built were provided with Westinghouse brakes alongside vacuum ejector braking. The Westinghouse pump is clearly visible ahead of the right-hand tank.   *T.G. Hepburn/Rail Archive Stephenson*

'L1' class No. E9011 at Shenfield on 26th June, 1948.   *H.C. Casserley*

Later members of the 'L1' class, BR Nos. 67740 to 67800, were fitted with steam brakes with a vacuum ejector for train braking. 'L1' class No. 67760, bearing the legend 'BRITISH RAILWAYS', rests outside Grantham shed on 22nd March, 1949.   *John P. Wilson/Rail Archive Stephenson*

'L1' class No. 67798.   *Peter Townend Collection*

'L1' class No. 67721 at Bishops Stortford shed on 15th April, 1957.

J.F. Davies/Rail Archive Stephenson

excessive bearing wear and high coupled wheel revolutions caused wear in the motion parts and connecting rods and, consequently, adversely affected the running costs and the availability of the locomotives.

Some of, if not all, these troubles can be ascribed to the very nature of fast suburban work. Eventually several 'L1s' were fitted with manganese steel axlebox lines which no doubt helped to overcome the 'wear and tear' problems.

These locomotives were allocated to Neasden as this depot was having difficulty in maintaining fast outer suburban services.

The 'L1' was not one of Thompson's most successful designs and although 100 of them were built, withdrawals began early in the dieselisation programme and the class became extinct in December 1962.

Dimensions 'L1'

Cylinders:	dia.	2 x 20 in. (some reduced to 18¾ in. in 1951)
	stroke	26 in.
Valve gear:	outside	Walschaert
	inside	
Max. cut-off in full gear		75%
Max. valve travel		6⅝ in.
Steam lap:	outside	1⅝ in.
	inside	
Piston valve dia.		10 in.
Coupled wheel dia.		5 ft 2 in.
Length of boiler barrel		
between tube plates		12 ft 2 in.
Heating surface:	firebox	138.5 sq. ft
	tubes and flues	1198.0 sq. ft
	superheater	284.0 sq. ft
Total heating surface		1,620.5 sq. ft
Grate area		24.24 sq. ft
Working pressure		225 lb./sq. in.
Tractive effort (85% boiler pressure)		32,080 lb.
Total adhesive weight		132,048 lb.
Weight of engine in working order		89 tons 9 cwt ('L1s' built by R. Stephenson & Hawthorn weighed 92 tons 17 cwt)
Coal capacity		4½ tons
Water capacity		2,630 galls
Brake type		Westinghouse brake and vacuum ejector

The 'K5' and 'B2'

The *Railway Gazette* of 28th September, 1945 contains an article headed 'Another LNER Locomotive Conversion'. It opens with a rather acid comment 'Yet another of the Gresley classes of three cylinder locomotives has been made the subject of Mr Thompson's reforms'. The writer is referring to the rebuilding of a 'K3' 2-6-0 locomotive and before considering this in detail, it is worthwhile reviewing how far Thompson had gone towards achieving his overall plans.

He had broadly divided the LNER locomotive types into three groups - new standard types, existing types that were considered worth maintaining until the end of their useful lives, and locomotives not included in either of the preceding groups, mostly of older design and whose duty could be transferred to one of the standard types. Details of Groups One and Two are shown below:

Group One - Standard types

Class	Description
'A1'	Express passenger - prototype rebuilt from original Gresley Pacific.
'A2'	Heavy passenger and freight prototype rebuilt from 2-8-2.
'B1'	New design with standard components.
'K1'	Mixed traffic - prototype rebuilt from 'K4' - standard components.
'O1'	Mineral - prototype rebuilt from Robinson 2-8-0.
'J11'	Freight - prototype rebuilt from Robinson 0-6-0.
'L1'	New design - standard components.
'Q1'	Heavy shunting tank - prototype rebuilt from Robinson 0-8-0.
'J50'	Medium shunting tank - prototype rebuilt from Gresely 0-6-0.

Group Two - Non-standard types

Class	Description
'A3'	Gresley Pacific as built.
'A4'	Streamlined Pacific as built.
'B17'	Gresley 'Sandringhams'. Cylinders and valve gear to be modified and to become 'B2' class. Identical with 'B1' but with 6 ft 8 in. coupled wheels.
'D49'	Gresley 'Hunts' and 'Shires'. Some experimental rebuilding carried out.
'B16'	Raven design - valve gear to be modified.
'K3'	Rebuilt to 'K5' as described.
'V2'	'Green Arrow' class as built.
'O4'	Robinson 2-8-0 - rebuilt to 'O1' as described.
'V1'	Gresley 3-cylinder tank locomotive.
'V3'	As 'V1' but with higher boiler pressure.

Thompson's new locomotives were built with simplicity of handling and maintenance in mind and on the principle that two cylinders should be used unless power requirements for any particular service were greater than two cylinders could reasonably supply. It will be seen from the table above that he had not overlooked the necessity to maintain the locomotives in Group Two and he took every opportunity to introduce standard parts into these locomotives with a view to post-war development. In following this outline, Thompson planned to reduce the 166 classes of LNER locomotives to 19.

The table below shows the classes of locomotives that were designed around basic features of 225 lb. per sq. in. boiler pressure, two outside cylinders of 20 in. diameter by 26 in. stroke and 10 in. piston valves.

Class	Type	Designation	Coupled wheel dia.	Remarks
'B1'	4-6-0	Mixed traffic	6 ft 2 in.	New design
'B2'	4-6-0	Express passenger	6 ft 8 in.	Rebuilt from 'Sandringham' 'B17s'
'O1'	2-8-0	Heavy freight	4 ft 8 in.	Rebuilt from Robinson GCR 2-8-0 ('O4')
'K1'	2-6-0	Goods and mixed traffic	5 ft 8 in.	New class – developed from Gresley 'K4'
'K5'	2-6-0	Mixed traffic	5 ft 8 in.	Rebuilt from Gresley 3-cylinder 'K3'
'L1'	2-6-4	Mixed traffic	5 ft 2 in.	New design

Thompson's standardization plans were incorporated in a series of books issued for internal use at Doncaster works between 1943 and 1946. As far as can be ascertained five were circulated and they indicate that there was some re-thinking of policy as time progressed.

Included in the early editions were proposals for the retention of the 'J72' tank locomotive, a Wilson Worsdell design originating with the North Eastern Railway in 1898 as a standard type, the introduction of a small 4-4-0 the 'D' class, the rebuilding of Gresley's three-cylinder 2-6-2 tank locomotive as the two-cylinder standard passenger tank and the rebuilding of the entire class of 'B16s'. In addition, the 'A1' and 'A3' Pacifics were to be given boilers of 250 lb./sq. in working pressure.

Subsequent editions were changed, presumably in the light of operating experience. The two-cylinder version of the 'V3' became the 'L1' 2-6-4 tank, the Gresley-designed 'J50' 0-6-0 tank replaced the 'J72' and after going to the trouble of preparing a detailed diagram of the proposed 4-4-0 for one edition, it was omitted from the next.

In the edition that included a diagram of the rebuilt *Great Northern*, the following notes are appended:

1. One A1 type engine is being converted to the ex-P2 cylinder arrangement. This engine will have an A4 boiler pressed to 250 lbs/sq. inch. It is hoped that the tests in Note 2 will provide a boiler common to all Type A engines.
2. So far, the P2 type and four V2 type engines have been built or converted to the 4-6-2 wheel arrangement. There are three different boilers in use on the ex-P2 type alone, including engine 10000. The performances of these engines are being observed in order that the best features of these existing boilers can be incorporated in one design carrying 250 lbs. pressure.

From the above, it is apparent that Thompson's standardization policies were well thought out and that he was prepared to amend and modify if necessary. The notes indicate that he regarded the rebuilding of the 'P2s' and the converting of the 'V2s' as partly experimental. On the other hand, one cannot help thinking that the 'L1' 2-6-4 tank locomotive was an example of standardization gone mad and that a two-cylinder version of the 'V3' might have been more successful.

The alternative inclusion and omission of the 4-4-0 or 'D' class is rather puzzling, but this design was no doubt based on a rebuild of 'D49/2' *The Morpeth*. This locomotive was one of a series introduced by Gresley in 1928 and were in turn a development of his 'D49' 'Shire' class, introduced in 1927.

The 1927 'D49s' were three-cylindered with Walschaert's/Gresley valve gear, and their successors, the 1928 'D49s', were fitted with Lentz rotary cam valve gear.

In practice, difficulties arose with the Lentz rotary cam mechanism, as it was not possible to provide a wide range of cut-offs and this limited locomotive performance. In 1938 Gresley fitted 'D49/2' *The Morpeth* with a modified form of rotary cam valve gear which allowed a full range of cut-off positions. This experiment was abandoned after Gresley's death and Thompson rebuilt *The Morpeth* with two inside cylinders of ex-Great Central 'Director' class pattern and piston valves operated by Stephenson link motion.

'D49/2' class 4-4-0 No. 62762 *The Fernie* arrives at Middlesbrough with a passenger train. These locomotives were fitted with Lentz rotary cam poppet valves. The earlier 'D49s', subsequently reclassified as 'D49/1', had piston valves and Walschaert's valve gear.

T.G. Hepburn/Rail Archive Stephenson

'D49/2' class 4-4-0 No. 365 *The Morpeth* after rebuilding into a 'D' class with inside cylinders and Stephenson valve gear.

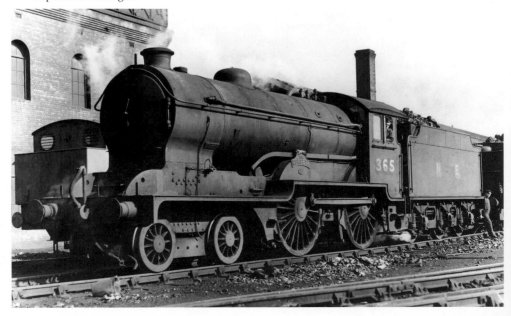

Opinions differ widely over the success of the rebuild. It spent most of its working life in the North Eastern Area, and has been variously described as 'a good engine by all accounts' to a 'melancholy failure'. Five rebuilds were authorised, but *The Morpeth* was the only one completed and it came to an unfortunate end after being involved in a light engine collision at Dragon Junction, near Harrogate. The front of the locomotive was damaged beyond economic repair, the remains towed to Darlington and were scrapped in November 1952.

To return to the remarks that opened this section, Thompson had reached the stage where he had developed a highly satisfactory 'general utility' locomotive, the 'B1', he had introduced a heavy freight locomotive, the 'O1', a heavy shunting tank locomotive, the 'Q1', a mixed traffic tank locomotive, the 'L1', and a 4-6-0 express passenger locomotive, the 'B2'. He was going ahead with his plans for his proposed Pacific but had not yet produced a 'lightweight' tender locomotive for miscellaneous work. With this in mind and with the experience gained from the conversion of the 'B3' and the 'B17', he rebuilt a Gresley 'K3' 2-6-0 and changed it from three-cylinder propulsion to two.

The 'K3' design originated with the Great Northern Railway, the first member of the class appearing in 1920. At the time, it was the largest 2-6-0 in the country and a large number of them - 183 - were produced after the formation of the LNER. The three cylinders were 18½ in. x 26 in., equipped with 8 in. piston valves and Gresley 2:1 gear for the inside cylinder. Boiler pressure was 180 lb. per sq. in. and the nominal tractive effort was 30,031 lb.

The company's official 'hand-out' on the conversion stated that it had been carried out to save maintenance costs. Admittedly, in eliminating the inside cylinder, a number of heavy moving parts had been removed, but Thompson equipped the locomotive with a 225 lb. per sq. in. boiler and two new outside cylinders of 20 in. x 26 in. to the standard pattern. This he had to do to maintain the tractive effort and to compensate for the loss of one cylinder. He fitted the locomotive with Walschaert's valve gear, details of which were also standard and common to the 'B1', 'O1' and 'L1' locomotives. Other considerations were a new driving axle, replacement of the Gresley double swing-link pony truck with one that was laterally sprung and re-balancing of the reciprocating parts. On the face of it, an expensive exercise.

The rebuilt locomotive was reclassified 'K5' and was the only member of its class. The impression of it that remains is that it became a rough-riding engine more quickly than did other two-cylinder tender engines of Thompson design. That he did not pursue the idea is significant. Instead, he used another Gresley 2-6-0, the 'K4', as the basis for his standard mixed traffic locomotive.

Gresley 'K3' class 2-6-0 No. 146 on an up slow goods train at Retford.   *Lens of Sutton Collection*

'K5' class 2-6-0 No. 1863 waiting for the road at Greenwood to pass through the two-track Hadley Wood-Potters Bar section with a down goods *circa* 1946/1947.
Robert Brookman/Rail Archive Stephenson

Dimensions 'K3' and 'K5'

		'K3'	'K5'
Cylinders:	dia.	3 x 18½ in.	2 x 20 in.
	stroke	26 in.	26 in.
Valve gear:	outside	Walschaert	Walschaert
	inside	Gresley	
Max. cut-off in full gear		75%	75%
Max. valve travel		6⅜ in.	6⅜ in.
Steam lap:	outside]	1½ in.	1½ in.
	inside]		
Piston valve dia.		8 in.	10 in.
Coupled wheel dia.		5 ft 8 in.	5 ft 8 in.
Length of boiler barrel			
between tube plates			11 ft 11⅞ in.
Heating surface:	firebox	182 sq. ft	182 sq. ft
	tubes and flues	1,719 sq. ft	1,719 sq. ft
	superheater	527 sq. ft	407 sq. ft
Total heating surface		2,428 sq. ft.	2,308 sq. ft
Grate area		28 sq. ft	28 sq. ft
Working pressure		180 lb./sq. in.	225 lb./sq. in.
Tractive effort (85% boiler pressure)		30,030 lb.	29,250 lb.
Total adhesive weight		134,400 lb.	137,200 lb.
Weight of engine and			
tender in working order		131 tons 14 cwt	123 tons 5 cwt
Coal capacity		7½ tons	7½ tons
Water capacity		4,200 galls	4,200 galls
Brake type		Vacuum	Steam and vacuum ejector

The section of the LNER that was formerly Great Eastern territory was handicapped by rigid loading restrictions originally imposed by the Civil Engineer's Department of the Great Eastern Railway, by limited platform clearances and by small turntables, and the Mechanical Engineer's Department had little option but to design locomotives accordingly.

Towards the end of World War I, meetings of the civil and mechanical engineers of the various railway companies were held in an attempt to reach uniform agreement on the subject of hammer blow and to work towards a range of standard locomotives in anticipation of the expected Nationalisation of the railways. When the decision was taken to amalgamate and not to nationalise, the meetings were discontinued, but by then the civil engineers had committed themselves and specified axle loadings. On this basis, Gresley formulated his 'big engine policy' and began a series of designs based on the permitted axle loadings of 20 tons, whilst the Great Eastern designers under A.J. Hill continued to err on the side of caution.

It was, therefore, almost inevitable that when Gresley became chief mechanical engineer of the LNER he would endeavour to improve the services in East Anglia by designing a locomotive that embodied all that he thought best, yet at the same time was within the Great Eastern section of limited axle loading and hammer blow. The result of these designs was the 'B17' 4-6-0 express passenger locomotive, a three-cylinder machine, with 6 ft 8 in. driving wheels and Gresley conjugated valve gear for the inside cylinder. Introduced in 1928

'B12' class 4-6-0 No. 8508 with ACFI feed which it carried on the top of its boiler from 1931 to 1941.   *Rail Archive Stephenson*

No. 8508 was rebuilt by Thompson to a 'B12/4' class in July 1943. We see the locomotive, by now carrying British Railways number 61508, at Kittybrewster shed on 3rd September, 1949.

J.M. Jarvis Online Transport Archive in assocoation with Rail Archive Stephenson

and built at intervals until 1937, the class eventually numbered 73 locomotives. The introduction of these locomotives - colloquially called the 'Sandringhams' - was no mean achievement by Sir Nigel Gresley.

The new class was augmented by Thompson's rebuilt 'B12s' and later by the rebuilt 'Claud Hamiltons', with the result that heavily-loaded trains were efficiently worked between Liverpool Street and the East Anglian holiday centres, such as Yarmouth and Harwich, and the service was greatly improved.

The 'B17s' were used on various parts of the LNER and were not restricted to East Anglia. Some of them were named after football clubs and as far as possible were allocated to depots near the clubs whose names they carried. The entire class did some very fine work and underwent various modifications but the locomotives were not in line with Thompson's policy and, when No. 2871 was due for heavy repairs, he carried out a major conversion by replacing all the 'non-standard' parts with those of the standard pattern. This involved the elimination of the inside cylinder with the Gresley valve gear, the provision of two new outside cylinders of the 20 in. x 26 in. type, a standard 100A 'B1' boiler, a new driving axle and new bogie. In all probability, the conversion of the 'B3', *Earl Haig*, from four cylinders to two prompted Thompson to turn his attention to the 'B17', regarding the former as the prototype. Whereas only one 'B3' was converted, a total of 10 'B17s' was rebuilt, these taking place as heavy repairs became due. Reclassified as 'B2s', they were in fact 6 ft 8 in. versions of the 'B1s', and were used, as had been the original 'B17s', on express passenger work in East Anglia.

No. 1871 was named *Manchester City* at the time of the rebuilding, but on completion was renamed *Royal Sovereign* and used on Royal Train working between King's Cross and Wolferton, the station for Sandringham.

The table comparing the dimensions of the original 'B17' and the rebuilt 'B2' shows how little departure there was from the basic design and there were very slight differences in external appearance.

As usual, Thompson was not without his critics. Coming, as the 'B17' conversion did, close on the heels of the 'K3' conversion, comparisons were made and the railway press of the day carried letters both for and against the conversions and Thompson's policy in general.

Amongst the arguments put forward against three-cylinder to two-cylinder conversion were greater hammer blow and a tendency to 'shouldering' that is, excessive lateral movement of the locomotive which transmits itself to the train and hence increases wear on the track. It was also argued that this shouldering would increase as the locomotive mileage increased. Thus any costs that might be saved by ease of maintenance and higher locomotive availability would be nullified by higher costs of track maintenance. These criticisms were answered to a certain extent by rebalancing the reciprocating parts and fitting a Thompson bogie in place of the Gresley double swing link type.

Any discussion of hammer blow, three-cylinder propulsion versus two, and rough riding in locomotives of comparable size and power is beset with pitfalls.

Generally, a three-cylinder locomotive was easier on the track that its two-cylinder counterpart, as there was a more even torque pattern. The 'B17s' were good riding locomotives when properly maintained, but roughened up considerably if neglected. It was not possible to offset this by including a rear

'B17' class 4-6-0 No. 2803 *Framlingham* climbs Brentwood Bank with the 10.00 am Liverpool Street-Harwich passenger service *circa* 1930.   *F.R. Hebron/Rail Archive Stephenson*

Framlingham at Stratford shed in 1947, by now carrying LNER No. 1603. It had been rebuilt into a 'B2' class two-cylinder locomotive with a 100A boiler in 1945. Note the ex-North Eastern Railway tender.   *E.V. Fry/Rail Archive Stephenson*

pony truck without sacrificing adhesion and increasing length, thus defeating the purpose of the design.

Similarly, the 'B2' gave a lively ride if not adequately maintained, and a two-cylinder locomotive was inclined to 'roughen up' more quickly than one with three cylinders - herein lies one of the weaknesses of most of Thompson's two-cylinder conversions. But any locomotive would give a rough ride when run down, particularly if the cab was unsupported by a pony truck.

The real virtue of the 'B2s' - if not their only virtue - was ease of maintenance and, to a lesser extent, the way in which some crews and shed staffs seem to have accepted them. One critic, commenting on the rebuild, wrote: 'What is better, to have an engine of moderate performance which is a psychological tonic to shed fitters, or a first class locomotive which only needs proper maintenance?'

This was written in November 1945, only six months after the end of World War II. Implicit in it is the rather naïve assumption that the end of hostilities meant an almost immediate return to pre-war standards of locomotive practice.

Thompson was under no such illusion, as the 'B17' to 'B2' rebuild shows. He attempted to adapt to suit current conditions at the same time planning for the future.

Dimensions 'B17' and 'B2'

		'B17'	'B2'
Cylinders:	dia.	3 x 17½ in.	2 x 20 in.
	stroke	26 in.	26 in.
Valve gear:	outside	Walschaert	Walschaert
	inside	Gresley	
Max. cut-off in full gear		65.7%	75%
Max. valve travel		5²¹⁄₃₂ in.	6²¹⁄₃₂ in.
Steam lap:	outside]	1⁷⁄₁₆ in.	1⅝ in.
	inside]	1⅝ in.	
Piston valve dia.		8 in.	10 in.
Coupled wheel dia.		6 ft 8 in.	6 ft 8 in.
Length of boiler barrel			
between tube plates		14 ft 0 in.	13 ft 11⅞ in.
Heating surface:	firebox	168 sq. ft	168 sq. ft
	tubes and flues	1,508 sq. ft	1,493 sq. ft
	superheater	344 sq. ft	344 sq. ft
Total heating surface		2,020 sq. ft	2,005 sq. ft
Grate area		27.5 sq. ft	27.9 sq. ft
Working pressure		200 lb./sq. in	225 lb./sq. in.
Tractive effort (85% boiler pressure)		25,380 lb.	24,863 lb.
Total adhesive weight		121,744 lb.	122,528 lb.
Weight of engine and			
tender in working order		116 tons 13 cwt	124 tons 18 cwt
depending on which tender used		129 tons 3 cwt	125 tons 10 cwt
Coal capacity		4 tons	7 tons
depending on which tender used		7½ tons	7½ tons
Water capacity		3,700-4,200 galls	4,200-4,700 galls
Brake type		Westinghouse and vacuum ejector or steam and vacuum ejector or vacuum	Steam and vacuum ejector

'B2' class No. 61671 *Royal Sovereign*, formerly 'B17' class *Manchester City* and rebuilt with a higher boiler pressure, two cylinders and 6 ft 8 in. driving wheels.

No. 61671 *Royal Sovereign* in immaculate condition with its white cab roof. It was used whenever possible on the Royal Train between Liverpool Street and Wolferton (for Sandringham).

'Great Northern'

In April 1922 Gresley, then locomotive superintendent of the Great Northern Railway, introduced the first two of the Pacific class of locomotives for which he was destined to become famous. The first, built at Doncaster and numbered 1470 was named *Great Northern*. It had a boiler that tapered from 6 ft 5 in. at the firebox to 5 ft 9 in. at the smokebox, boiler pressure of 180 lb. per sq. in., three cylinders with Gresley derived motion for the valve gear of the inside cylinder, and all three cylinders driving onto the middle coupled axle.

It should perhaps be remembered that locomotives as big as these Pacifics had not previously been built and that the class as a whole was notable for the sheer size of its members. In the light of operating experience, considerable improvements were made to cylinders and valve details and low pressure boilers were replaced with boilers of a higher pressure. The original locomotives were heavy on coal, inclined to be sluggish, but capable of good performances in skilled hands.

Between 1922 and 1935 79 non-streamlined Pacifics were built and members of the first batch, classified as 'A1', were converted as described above and re-classified as 'A3'. (To pre-empt a plethora of letters, there were, by a quirk, 80 non-streamlined Pacifics. No. 2744 *Grand Parade* was damaged beyond repair in the accident at Castlecary on 10th December, 1937 and an order was placed for a new 'A3' also to be called *Grand Parade* - it was completed before the original was cut up.)

Great Northern was a useful performer, but not an outstanding member of its class, although by virtue of its pride of place, it was regarded with affection by railwaymen and enthusiasts alike. Re-numbered 4470 on Grouping, it was not converted to an 'A3' with a 220 lb. boiler, as were most of the original 'A1' class and in 1944 it entered Doncaster works, emerging on 25th September, 1945 completely transformed. That the rebuild was controversial is beyond dispute and never in the history of the Country's railways has the conversion of a locomotive generated more heat than light and consigned its designer to perdition.

In *British Pacific Locomotives*, C.J. Allen describes the transformation as 'hideous and calculated to make its designer turn in his grave'. Mr Allen also makes the point that *Great Northern* was the pioneer Pacific, the original of 1922, but the project is worthy of more than the cursory examination that it has hitherto received.

In *Thompson and Peppercorn - Locomotive Engineers* Col H.C.B. Rogers states, 'Out of all of them [the remaining 'A1s'] to the horror of everyone who had been connected with Doncaster, Thompson selected the pioneer of the class'. He then goes on to quote J. F.Harrison, 'All the time Thompson had at the back of his mind a determination to undermine Gresley's reputation and what better way than to take the first Pacific that Gresley built and re-build it'.

O. S. Nock is a little more circumspect. In *LNER Steam* he writes about the consternation that ensued , 'when she was re-built out of all recognition' and he continues, 'Among locomotive lovers harsh words were used about Thompson and all his works and comments not greatly watered down appeared in some of the enthusiast journals'.

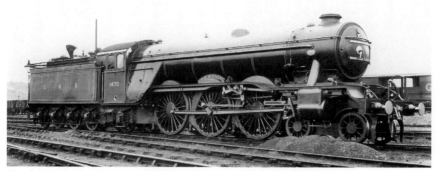

Gresley 'A1' class 4-6-2 No. 1470 *Great Northern* at Hornsey in 1923.
W. Beckerlegge/Rail Archive Stephenson

In this context Peter Townend commented dryly, 'CMEs do not consider enthusiasts but technical facts'. The January/February 1946 issue of *Railway Magazine* devotes one page to a description of the re-build with a before and after photograph.

Thompson was constantly trying to improve performance and to standardize and his work on No. 4470 shows to what length he was prepared to go to achieve this end. His selection of 4470 as a prototype for improving Pacific performance was perhaps a psychological error, but his choice was limited as only six of the original 'A1s' were left when he was authorized to proceed with his plans. Had he chosen one of the others, say No. 4473, then the outcry might not have been as loud as it was. It is the considered opinion of one member of the team which worked on No. 4470 that Thompson selected it, not so much because in his mind it personified Gresley and therefore by rebuilding it he was symbolically destroying him, but because he - Thompson - felt that if his ideas and designs were successful, then it was fitting that No. 4470 should be the first locomotive to embody the improvements that were envisaged.

Great Northern as rebuilt by Thompson, without smoke deflectors and with straight nameplates.

At the time that the rebuild was started, steel was in short supply and licences had to be obtained for major repairs and for new construction. The Ministry of Supply was prepared to grant the necessary authority for the former but not for the latter and thus, the *Great Northern* project was scheduled as a rebuild. In fact, the original locomotive was quietly dismantled and that which came out as *Great Northern* was not only built in the new erecting shop, but was a completely new engine, the only parts of the original that were used being the wheel centres, some of the axles and the tender. It was, of course, very different from its predecessor. As with all Thompson three-cylinder locomotives, divided drive was used with separate valve gear for each cylinder but strangely, the connecting rods were not of equal length - there was 10 inch difference in length between the two outside connecting rods and that of the inside, thus necessitating the repositioning of the bogie 2 ft 8 in. forward of its position on the original 'A1'. In a letter to the author, E.S. Cox writes: 'I do not think that Thompson's main object was to undo all Gresley's work. In two matters however he was quite determined, firstly to do away with the conjugated gear, and secondly to use two instead of three cylinders for all the medium- and small-sized locos. In these trends he was abundantly right and it is a pity that this entirely correct thinking got tangled up with non-sequiturs like the necessity for equal length of connecting rod'. Perhaps by the time that No. 4470 was undergoing conversion, Thompson had realised that the necessity for equal length connecting rods was a non sequitur?

The diameters of all three cylinders were reduced from 20 to 19 inches and an 'A4'-type boiler (diagram 107) was fitted. This brought with it an increase in boiler pressure and size that considerably offset the cylinder reduction and increased weight in terms of tractive effort.

No. 4470 emerged from Doncaster works painted in Royal Blue and lined out in red, this being the standard livery of the former Great Eastern Railway, and its appearance immediately gave rise to adverse comment. Some of this was perhaps justified as photographs of the 1922 'A1' and 1945 version show - but appearances are a matter of opinion and the Chapelon-designed French locomotives indicate that too much weight should not be placed on them.

The Gresley 'A1' and 'A3' locomotives were introduced at a time when a locomotive was expected to look graceful : in the war years the emphasis was on utility. No. 4470, with its rimless double chimney, raised running place, short cab side sheets, long smoke box and repositioned cylinders certainly looked very different from the original. There were valid reasons for trying some of these features - absence of splashers facilitated maintenance and the rimless chimney was thought to help in preventing eddy currents and lift the exhaust.

In *Locomotives of the LNER, Standardization and Renumbering* published by the LNER in 1947, O.S. Nock states that No. 4470 was to be streamlined as would future members of the class. In a letter to the author, Peter Townend writes, 'I think that it was always intended to use the smoke deflection asset of the streamlined front on the 'A1s' when built after the war and money was allocated in the order. Streamlining was as much about smoke deflection as fashion and saving power at speed. It was the culmination of Doncaster's various trials in smoke deflection and of course was used on the 'P2' for this reason'.

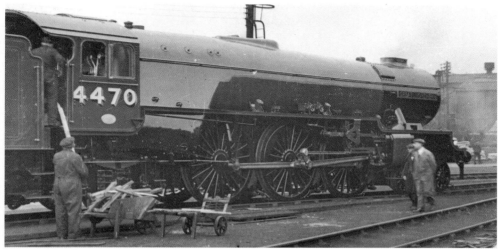

Top left: The rebuilt *Great Northern* under construction in the new erecting shop at Doncaster.
P. Wright

Above: Tinder is passed into the cab of No. 4470 in preparation for firelighting at Doncaster.
Peter Townend Collection

Below: Two fitters stand next to the newly-rebuilt No. 4470 at Doncaster.
Peter Townend Collection

Bottom left: The cab of No. 4470 *Great Northern* after rebuilding showing the Great Central-type
regulator handle, steam brake and electric lighting.   *LNER*

It seems that wartime conditions precluded No. 4470 from being equipped with a streamlined nose, hence the rimless chimney and the newly-formed Railway Executive vetoed any form of streamlining in spite of Doncaster's success in overcoming the problem of drifting exhaust.

Was the expense and work involved justified? From an operating point of view it undoubtedly was. The new locomotive was considerably more powerful that its predecessor and incorporated design features that gave it a distinct advantage. It had a rocking grate with hopper ashpan, electric lighting powered by a Metropolitan Vickers stub axle generator driven by the second bogie wheel on the left-hand side (subsequently changed for a Stokes steam driven turbo generator) and the lights were not only in the conventional headlamp position, but at various places in the cab.

On the 'road' the locomotive steamed very well and ran very freely due to no small measure to the incorporation of a Kylchap double blast-pipe chimney. The original 'A1s' required skilled firing to make them steam well, but the new version was just the opposite and its capacity for steaming was enormous.

Thompson did not use a Gresley double beat regulator valve with a vertical pull-out handle operating on both sides of the cab, as the valve had been

LNER No. 4470 *Great Northern* sports its large smoke deflectors.   *LNER*

troublesome during the war and had given rise to continuous blow-through. Instead, he used a horizontal slide valve type with a single handle working across the firebox backplate.

But this type of regulator valve also proved itself to be unsatisfactory in service and occasionally stuck open with un-nerving consequences. This happened when the locomotive was on a King's Cross-Doncaster run with an intermediate stop at Peterborough. The train was checked by a calling-on signal on the down platform and almost brought to a halt. The signal was cleared just before the train stopped and the driver, anxious to get the whole of his train into the platform before his passengers began to alight, opened the regulator, probably against the brakes, and the valve stuck open, *Great Northern* slipped for several minutes, wearing away the rails, and following this incident, with its subsequent upheaval, the regulator valve was changed for a single seat balanced type.

There is no denying that *Great Northern* had its faults. It suffered from leakage of steam at the front end, due to difficulty in keeping the exhaust steam pipe joints tight, and it had a history of fractured smokebox frames and rivets, but it should be remembered that *Great Northern* was a prototype. In the period of its construction the tendency was to build 6 ft 2 in. wheel locomotives for mixed traffic work and Thompson was planning ahead for the time when there would be a return to fast running and a consequent demand for 6 ft 8 in. Pacifics. Thus, *Great Northern* should be considered as the first step towards a final version of a 6 ft 8 in. driving wheel locomotive, which the Peppercorn 'A1s' were. Had not the precedent for this been set? The Gresley 'A1s' were the first step towards the 'A4s', over 30 years separating the original and final forms.

In the brief section on the locomotive in *British Pacific Locomotives* reference is made to the fact that when in 1946 trials were held to assess the condition of the track in relation to a return to pre-war schedules, an 'A4' was chosen to work the train and not *Great Northern*. The implications here are what the reader cares to make of them: the facts are that *Great Northern* was allocated to Doncaster at the time, that the train was to be worked out of King's Cross, and as King's Cross MPD had a stud of 'A4s', it was convenient from an operating point of view to use one of them. No doubt there are those who like to imagine the Chairman, when authorizing the trials, specifying that *Great Northern* was to be used, only to be put off by the operating people, but no such evidence, apocryphal or otherwise, exists.

Finally , I am indebted to Mr O.S. Nock for permission to use the following account of a footplate run on *Great Northern*. It is taken from his *British Steam Locomotives at Work* (Ian Allan 1967).

From the Gresley 'A1' class it is appropriate to turn to the Thompson alterations and just before Easter 1946 I rode the rebuilt *Great Northern* on the Aberdonian. A relief train preceded us at 7.10 pm; and though our train was not unduly heavy, the accommodation was packed almost to the limit. Our gross load of 440 tons behind the tender was medium by pre-war East Coast standards, and while not providing a test of all-out haulage capacity for the new engine, it gave ample opportunities for the crew to display with what ease and economy such a train load could be operated at an average speed equal to that of the pre-war 1.20 pm 'Scotsman'. Of course, it must be conceded that the rebuilt 4470 was almost new from the shops, and that she had a nominal tractive effort of 37,397 lb. against the 29,835 lb. of the Gresley 'A1' class.

No. 4470 *Great Northern* crosses Welwyn viaduct with the up 'Royal Mail'. *Colling Turner*

It was raining steadily as we started away, and we did not finally run into fine weather until nearing Peterborough. The cab layout is generally the same as that of the class 'A3' and 'A4' Pacifics, except that No. 4470 was fitted experimentally with a single regulator handle working across the firebox backplate. This was the one feature of the engine that did not seem very popular. The Flaman speed recorder was installed and working, though the chart was not inserted, and a graphic record was not taken.

Driver Williams opened up gradually in starting out of King's Cross. In the old days it seemed invariably a case of 'all or nothing' with the East Coast expresses on 'A1', 'A3' and 'A4' classes alike. Despite the difficult road through the tunnels, drivers would open out almost at once to full regulator, and often the cut-off had not been reduced much below 50 per cent by the time Belle Isle was passed. Williams used 45 per cent from the point of entering the first tunnel and the readings taken from the steam chest pressure gauge show that the regulator was very far from full open; 140 lb. per sq. in. through the first tunnel, a little more at Belle Isle; 180 from Holloway summit; and finally up to a full 240 at Wood Green. As on the 'A4' class it was scarcely possible to detect any difference between boiler and steam chest pressure when the regulator was full open.

We went very quietly and easily up to Potters Bar, on no more than 18 per cent cut-off, and then at Marshmoor, the regulator was brought right back and we worked rapidly up to 69½ mph north of Hatfield. The riding of the engine was smooth and effortless, and on straight open stretches, where the influence of curves and switches was absent, she was plumb steady although pleasantly buoyant. On a cold wet evening conditions were not favourable for good visibility, but the deflector shields, however unprepossessing they may look, kept the clouds of lightly drifting exhaust steam clear of the cab look-out. We passed Hatfield 20 minutes early on the easy allowance of 30 minutes then in force, but got a double yellow near Welwyn Garden City, and this was prelude to a slack to 40 mph over Digswell Viaduct.

In comparing this run with pre-war practice it must be remembered that there was an overall speed limit of 70 mph in force on the East Coast main line at the time, and that the Aberdonian was allowed 123 minutes for the 105½ miles from King's Cross to Grantham, against the 114 minutes of the pre-war 1.20 pm 'Scotsman' when I rode on *Royal Lancer*. This of course, called for much easier working, and on passing Stevenage and entering upon the famous racing stretch down to the Ouse valley, the regulator was eased right back to the drifting position, giving no more than 40 psi in the steam chest: the cut-off was 15 per cent. It would have been interesting to see what speed was attained in such conditions; but we encountered adverse signals at Hitchin and again at St Neot's, and a slack for permanent was relaying near Huntingdon. It was nevertheless significant of the easiness of the schedule that despite all these, we still passed Peterborough slightly ahead of time, in 87½ minutes from King's Cross.

For some little time we had been travelling with lights in the cab. It was evident that very great care had been devoted to the layout of the electric lamps and their shading, and that the illumination of the various steam and vacuum gauges, and the water level indicators was most effective. At the same time the retention of the square front cab of the 'A10' Pacific, from which No. 4470 was rebuilt, robs the engine of an advantage possessed by the 'A4' and the 'V2' classes. After dark, various objects in the cab lit by the glare of the fire are reflected in the look-out glass, whereas on engines with the wedge-shaped cab front the angle of the look-out avoids reflection altogether. This point was particularly noticeable when I transferred from No. 4470 to an 'A4' at Grantham.

After Peterborough, *Great Northern* was opened out to a greater extent than previously, with regulator practically full open and 18 per cent cut-off, and steam chest varying from 205 to 240 psi. Working thus she gave an excellent account of herself, attaining 68 mph on the gradual rise that leads on to the 1-in-200 gradient of the Stoke bank. However, at Peterborough, a British Liberation Army leave special had been sandwiched in between the advance and the main section of the 'Aberdonian' and just as we were going very well up the 1 in 200 bank, Corby distant was sighted at caution. The home signal was lowered only to our close approach and we drew slowly through the station to a stand at the advanced starter.

The stop lasted for just 1½ minutes, and from this dead start we made an excellent climb up the 1 in 178 to Stoke. Cut-off was 30 per cent at first, later reduced to 25 per cent and finally to 20 per cent. In accelerating this 440 ton load to 43 mph in 2¾ miles an output equivalent to at least 1,650 draw-bar horse power was involved. At a moderate speed and by means a long cut-off this was an impressive manifestation of what the new engines could do. From Stoke summit, an easy run downhill, and further adverse signals did not prevent us from reaching Grantham less than 2 minutes late. The net time was 114½ minutes, roughly equal to the old 1.20 pm schedule.

The Thompson engine had, taken all in all, given a good account of herself, but she was working under relatively easy conditions....

BR No. 60113 *Great Northern* in a spot of trouble with its leading axle off the road in York yard in June 1962.   *C.K. Field Archive*

Dimensions 'A1'

		Gresley 'A1' (Reclassified 'A10')	Thompson 'A1'
Cylinders:	dia.	3 x 20 in.	3 x 19 in.
	stroke	26 in.	26 in.
Valve gear:	outside	Walschaert	Walschaert
	inside	Gresley	Walschaert
Max. cut-off in full gear		65%	75%
Max. valve travel		5¾ in.	6 in.
Steam lap:	outside	1⅝ in.	1⅝ in.
	inside	1 in.	1⅝ in.
Piston valve dia.		8 in.	10 in.
Coupled wheel dia.		6 ft 8 in.	6 ft 8 in.
Length of boiler barrel between tube plates		19 ft	17 ft 11¾ in.
Heating surface:	firebox	215 sq. ft	231.2 sq. ft
	tubes and flues	2,715 sq. ft	2,345.1 sq. ft
	superheater	525 sq. ft	748.9 sq. ft
Total heating surface		3,455 sq. ft	3,325 sq. ft
Grate area		41.25 sq. ft	41.25 sq.ft
Working pressure		180 lb./sq. in	250 lb./sq. in.
Tractive effort (85% boiler pressure)		29,835 lb.	37,397 lb.
Total adhesive weight		60 tons	66 tons
Weight of engine and tender in working order		150 tons 7 cwt	159 tons 8 cwt
Coal capacity		9 tons	9 tons
Water capacity		5,000 galls	5,000 galls
Brake type		Vacuum ejector	Vacuum ejector

The 'K1'

In 1937, during Thompson's time as mechanical engineer, Darlington, Gresley introduced a 2-6-0 tender locomotive, the 'K4', designed specifically for the West Highland line. This particular stretch of track, steeply graded in places, winds and twists its way from Craigendoran Junction, near Glasgow, over the peaty wastes of Rannoch Moor to Fort William, thence to Mallaig by way of Lochielside and Glenfinnan. The area through which the latter part of this route lies is rich with historical associations of the 1745 Stuart Rebellion and presents what is considered by many people to be the best in Scottish scenery.

Operationally, however, the view is somewhat different. On a line of communication to an attractive tourist area, traffic was heavy during the season, imposing burdens on the running department and on the locomotives in use in the mid-1930s. These included former North British Railway 'Glen' type 4-4-0s introduced in 1913 by W.P. Reid, and Gresley 'K2' 2-6-0s sent to the West Highland line in 1924/25. On trains of over 200 tons, double-heading had to be used and in an attempt to overcome some of these operating diffuclties, the 'K4s' came into being. They were sturdy and compact engines, having a high tractive effort and capable of handling trains of 300 tons. They were equipped with three 18½ in. x 26 in. cylinders driving 5 ft 2 in. coupled wheels, piston valves, and Gresley derived motion for the inside cylinder. In keeping with the area in which they worked, they were given delightful Scottish names, and a total of six were built at Darlington in 1937 and 1938. They performed very usefully, but were expensive to maintain due, to a certain extent, to their small wheels combined with their ability to run fast on downhill and on level stretches of the track. In view of this and the fact they were designed for a particular job on a section of line at the extremity of the system, they hardly fitted into Thompson's overall schemes.

Similarly, the fleet of 'J39' 0-6-0 locomotives with which Gresley had endowed the LNER did not fit into Thompson's standardization plans, but there were 289 of them built at intervals between 1926 and 1941. They were equipped with Stephenson link motion operating valves of the two inside cylinders and had a high power output. This gave rise to certain maintenance problems associated with weaknesses in the design of the cross-head and big-end fastenings. Another difficulty experienced with the 'J39s' was the running restriction placed on the class by the chief civil engineer by virtue of its high leading axle loading of 19 tons 11 cwt. So, with the end of the war in sight and Thompson's anxiety to see his policies carried through, he rejected the 'J39s' as an acceptable mixed traffic type and instead, when 'K4' *MacCailin Mor* (correct Gaelic spelling is 'MacCailein Mor', the title of the Chief of the Argyll Campbells) was due for heavy repairs he carried out an extensive rebuild as the basis for future goods and mixed traffic locomotive.

As might be expected, the rebuilt 'K4', reclassified 'K1', was considerably simplified. As far as possible, standard parts were fitted, including two outside cylinders of 20 in. x 26 in. dimensions and to the same pattern as those fitted to the 'B1', 'L1' and 'O1' classes, and the same type of pony truck as supplied for the 'L1s' and 'O1s'. By eliminating the inside cylinder with its Gresley derived motion and equipping the outside cylinders with Walschaert's valve gear, the whole of the running gear was placed outside the frames, giving maximum accessibility. One interesting point is that Thompson did not fit a single-bar crosshead to the 'K1' but reverted to the double-bar type as fitted to the 'B1' and 'B2'. For some obscure reason Thompson had opted for a single-bar type for his 'L1' 2-6-4 tank engine - it was not a particularly successful innovation.

One effect of the rebuild was a reduction of 11 per cent in the tractive effort of the locomotive, but even so it was still higher than that of the 'J39' and it had a lower leading coupled axle loading, made possible by the use of the pony truck. Thus, Thompson attempted to solve two problems - to eliminate two classes of locomotives, one numerically small, the other numerically large, but both having special problems of availability and maintenance, and to provide a suitable alternative. It will be recalled that he had previously rebuilt a Gresley 'K3' 2-6-0 so that when the 'K1' was put into service, there were two prototype 2-6-0s upon which a standard class could be based. In the event, the 'K1' proved to be a very satisfactory locomotive and it was left to Thompson's successor, A.H. Peppercorn, to complete the programme with the introduction in 1949 of his 'K1' class, based largely on Thompson's modified 'K4'. Eventually, 70 'K1s'

Gresley 'K4' class No. 3442 *The Great Marquess* takes water at Crianlarich while working a Fort William-Glasgow (Queen Street) passenger train.   *T.G. Hepburn/Rail Archive Stephenson*

One member of the 'K4' class was rebuilt by Thompson in 1945 as a two-cylinder locomotive and was reclassified 'K1/1'. The rebuilt engine, *MacCailin Mor*, carrying British Railways No. 61997, shunts at Fort William in June 1954.   *E.V. Fry/Rail Archive Stephenson*

were built and with the 'B1s', shared the distinction of being amongst the last British Railways steam locomotives to be withdrawn from service.

The Stephenson Locomotive Society's 'Three Dales Tour' in May 1967 was hauled by 'K1' No. 62005 through Swaledale, Teesdale and Weardale (*see page 138*). The engine had been very well prepared by Hartlepool's motive power depot and was the ideal choice for the types of route traversed - the low axle loading and leading pony truck enabled the tour to penetrate into some very fine countryside. The organization was excellent and it seemed as though No. 62005 herself entered into the spirit of things. Despite generous use of the whistle, particularly along the Catterick Camp line, there was always plenty of steam in hand and although the engine was not stretched in any way, she responded to the demands of an unusual working in a very satisfactory manner. For some passengers, it was the last steam journey on British Rail and was made memorable by the performance of a well-designed locomotive.

Dimensions 'K4' and 'K1'

		'K4'	*'K1'*
Cylinders:	dia.	3 x 18½ in.	2 x 20 in.
	stroke	26 in.	26 in.
Valve gear:	outside	Walschaert	Walschaert
	inside	Gresley	
Max. cut-off in full gear		65%	75%
Max. valve travel		5⅝ in.	6⅝ in.
Steam lap:	outside	1⅝ in.	1⅝ in.
	inside	1 11/16 in.	
Piston valve dia.		8 in.	10 in.
Coupled wheel dia.		5 ft 2 in.	5 ft 2 in.
Length of boiler barrel between tube plates		11 ft 7⅛ in.	11 ft 7⅜ in.
Heating surface:	firebox	168 sq. ft	168 sq. ft
	tubes and flues	1,253.6 sq. ft	1,240 sq. ft
	superheater	310 sq. ft	300 sq. ft
Total heating surface		1,731.6 sq. ft	1,708 sq. ft
Grate area		27.5 sq. ft	27.9 sq. ft
Working pressure		200 lb./sq. in	225 lb./sq. in.
Tractive effort (85% boiler pressure)		36,598 lb.	32,081 lb.
Total adhesive weight		129,696 lb.	127,344 lb.
Weight of engine and tender in working order		112 tons 8 cwt	111 tons 1 cwt
Coal capacity		5½ tons	5½ tons
Water capacity		3,500 galls	3,500 galls
Brake type		Vacuum	Steam and vacuum ejector

The 'A2/3'

May 1946 was a significant month for the LNER. It saw completion at Doncaster works of the first of Thompson's Pacifics built to new designs and, apart from being the company's first brand new Pacific for eight years, was the 2,000th locomotive to be constructed at Doncaster.

An official photograph of No. 500.   *LNER*

The cabside of No. 500 displaying the plate showing the build date of 1946.
                                                    National Railway Museum

The emergence of the locomotive - numbered 500 under the 1946 renumbering scheme - came only a few weeks before Thompson retired and was, therefore, almost the climax to his career. It is easy to suspect him of a subtle piece of timing, particularly as the engine subsequently bore his name. It has been darkly hinted that works numbers were rearranged to accommodate the event - 'gerrymandering' was the expression used - and this may or may not be true, but it would be somewhat out of character as Thompson never actively sought publicity. In any case, he had been set a precedent: was not the 100th Pacific built at Doncaster named *Sir Nigel Gresley*?

To avoid confusion, a word here about classification. It will be remembered that the rebuilt *Great Northern* became classified as 'A1', the remaining low pressure Gresley 'Pacifics' being reclassified 'A10'. It was then Thompson's intention to classify his new Pacifics, of which No. 500 was the prototype, as 'A2', the modified 'V2' locomotives as 'A2/1' and the rebuilt 'Cock o' the North' class as 'A2/2', the Gresley Pacifics remaining as 'A3' and 'A4'.

What in fact happened was the 'A2' classification became 'A2/3' after Thompson had retired, and his successor A.H. Peppercorn introduced a 6 ft 2 in. Pacific which was classified as 'A2' and a 6 ft 8 in. Pacific, classified as 'A1'. In the minds of most people, the final version of Thompson's 'Pacific' was always known as the 'A2/3' and this is the classification that will be used hereafter.

Fifteen 'A2/3s' were built and they are generally held to be Thompson's most successful 'Pacific' design. They were largely based on the converted 'Cock o' the North' designs and were fitted with self-cleaning smokeboxes, hopper ashpans, rocking grates, BTH speed recorder and the prototype had electric lighting. Instead of 'banjo' domes, the 'A2/3s' had normal domes without the steam collector extension.

The traditional Gresley cab replaced the faired version and tenders similar to Gresley's high-sided non-corridor type were provided.

It will be noticed from the table (*page 116*) that the 'A2/3' was fitted with three cylinders of 19 in. stroke, 10 in. piston valves and a boiler of 250 lb./sq. in. working pressure. It also had a Kylchap double blast pipe and chimney and these features gave it its free steaming and running characteristics.

Extensive use was made of welding in the construction, and the quadrant link bracket, main-frame stays and the bogie frame stays and horns were fabricated. The bogie was, of course, of the Thompson side-support pattern.

The drive was divided between the leading and middle coupled axles and each cylinder had its independent set of Walschaert's valve gear, with connecting rods of equal length, necessitating the staggered cylinder layout.

Careful attention was paid to balancing. The crank axle and middle big-end were balanced completely within the extensions to the crank webs and 35 per cent of the reciprocating parts were balanced, distributed amongst the three pairs of coupled wheels.

On occasions the 'A2/3s' put up some remarkable performances, one of which is recorded in Mr C.J. Allen's *British Pacific Locomotives*, and shows a maximum speed of 89/90 mph at Thirsk. The locomotive was No. 60524 *Herringbone*, with a gross train load of 380 tons. Mr Allen states that this

No. 500 *Edward Thompson* in immaculate condition in early British Railways' days.

Peter Townened Collection

Detail of driving wheels and valve gear of No. 511 *Airborne*.   *LNER*

performance is superior to that of 'A2/2' *Earl Marischal*, mentioned in an earlier chapter, and described it as 'the most astonishing run that I have ever known in the north-bound direction between York and Darlington'. Praise indeed!

Somewhat less remarkable are the two runs recorded by Mr F.G. Cockman, but they do illustrate the day-to-day performances of the 'A2/3s'.

11th May, 1960
Train:	11.23 am Birmingham to Newcastle
Locomotive:	'A2' Pacific No. 60516 *Hycilla*
Load:	Tare - 272 tons; loaded 285 tons

Miles	Station	Schedule	Actual	Speed
0.00	York	0.0	0.0 sigs	
5.55	Beningborough		12.01	63
9.75	Tollerton		15.54	66
11.20	Alne		17.09	70
13.35	Raskelf		18.52	75
16.10	Pilmoor		21.01	77
18.00	Sessay		22.29	78
22.20	Thirsk		25.45	77
26.50	Otterington		29.14	74
29.95	Northallerton		32.02	74
33.75	Danby Wiske		34.56	79
37.20	Cowton		37.51	71
38.95	Eryholme		39.23 pws	68
41.55	Croft Spa		42.21	43
44.10	Darlington	47.0	46.15	

11th May, 1960
Train:	4.25 pm ex-Darlington (3.30 pm ex-Newcastle)
Locomotive:	'A2' Pacific No. 60517 *Ocean Swell*
Load:	Tare - 274 tons; loaded 290 tons

Miles	Station	Schedule	Actual	Speed
0.00	Darlington	0.0	0.0	
2.55	Croft Spa		4.42	53
5.15	Eryholme		7.39	54
6.90	Cowton		9.28	62
10.35	Danby Wiske		12.40	66
14.15	Northallerton		16.03	68
17.60	Otterington		19.02	70
21.90	Thirsk		22.32	74
26.10	Sessay		25.58	73
28.00	Pilmoor		27.29	75
30.75	Raskelf		29.39	76
32.90	Alne		31.21	76
34.35	Tollerton		32.29	76½
38.55	Beningborough		35.48	77
44.10	York	43.0	42.22	

Edward Thompson is seen at King's Cross carrying its BR No. 60500.   *C.K. Field Archive*

'A2/3' class 4-6-2 No. 60523 *Sun Castle* on the turntable at King's Cross shed on 23rd September, 1950.   *British Railways*

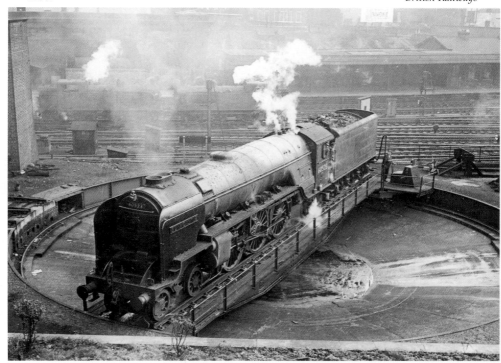

In considering these runs it is well to remember that the 'A2/3s' had coupled wheels of only 6 ft 2 in. diameter.

Although we have seen that the locomotives could - and did - steam well and were capable of outstanding performances, it is ironical that they were difficult to maintain, particularly as Thompson was greatly concerned with maintenance, orthodoxy and standardization.

His preoccupation with divided drive, equal length connecting rods and independent sets of valve gear for each cylinder gave rise to problems that were certainly not encountered on Gresley's Pacifics.

The staggered cylinder arrangement of the Thompson front end placed the inside cylinder where on the Gresley Pacifics there was a front frame bracing member. As it was not possible to accommodate this, the frame was inherently weaker at the front and needed very careful attention. Neglect resulted in loose smokebox rivets, saddle bolts that sheared and dropped out, cylinders that worked loose and generally rough riding.

What was potentially a more serious source of trouble was the middle eccentric. For satisfactory functioning, it relied upon adequate and frequent lubrication by the engine crews, but it was a long stretch to the oil containers. Failures of the eccentric were by no means commomplace, but so far as reliability is concerned, Gresley's 2:1 valve gear had the edge on Thompson's arrangement, providing that undue emphasis is not placed on even distribution of work amongst the three cylinders with its subsequent imbalance of forces.

In his efforts to eliminate the Gresley 2:1 valve gear as a source of maintenance difficulties, it seems that Thompson transferred the problem from one part of the locomotive to another.

In summarising Thompson's Pacific programme, we must not overlook the fact that the locomotives ran freely, steamed well and that the various types could do a better job than those that they replaced. They could even match the 'A4s' in performance until the latter class was fitted with Kylchap double blast pipes. Neither must we overlook the design faults already mentioned and it is an undisputed fact that these faults were carried forward with each successive design.

Thompson's 'Pacifics' suffered from emotional prejudices and these militate against objective assessment. An illustration of this point occurred when No. 60113 *Great Northern* was sent to King's Cross from Doncaster, only to be returned within a short time. The oft-repeated interpretation of this incident is that 'Top Shed' got rid of the engine because it was No. 60113 and that the depot staff wanted nothing to do with it.

It was, in fact, returned because a request for a locomotive was received; as No. 60113 was a 'one off' so far as the King's Cross maintenance facilities were concerned, it was logical to send it back.

One wonders just how many such apocryphal anti-Thompson stories could be demolished by probing beneath the surface.

Dimensions 'A2/3'

Cylinders:	dia.	3 x 18½ in.
	stroke	26 in.
Valve gear:	outside	Walschaert
	inside	Walschaert
Max. cut-off in full gear		75%
Max. valve travel		6¾ in.
Steam lap:	outside]	1⅝ in.
	inside]	
Piston valve dia.		10 in.
Coupled wheel dia.		6 ft 2 in.
Length of boiler barrel		
between tube plates		16 ft 11⅜ in.
Heating surface:	firebox	245.3 sq. ft
	tubes and flues	2,216.07 sq. ft
	superheater	679.67 sq. ft
Total heating surface		3,141.04 sq. ft
Grate area		50 sq. ft
Working pressure		250 lb./sq. in.
Tractive effort (85% boiler pressure)		40,340 lb.
Total adhesive weight		147,840 lb.
Weight of engine and		
tender in working order		161 tons 17 cwt
Coal capacity		9 tons
Water capacity		5,000 galls
Brake type		Steam and vacuum ejector

1946 Renumbering Scheme

Under an 'edict' 106 pages long and dated December 1943, Thompson proposed to rationalise the numbering of the entire stock of LNER locomotives. It was not, however, until early in 1946 that his proposals were put into operation, largely due to the fact that the mechanics of carrying them out were not possible under wartime conditions.

In theory, the idea was simple enough and is set out below:

Locomotive types	Numbers
All 4-6-2 and 2-6-2 ('V2') tender engines	1-999
All 4-6-0, 2-6-0 and 2-6-2 ('V4') tender engines	1000-1999
All 4-4-2, 4-4-0 and 2-4-0 tender engines	2000-2999
All 2-8-0, 0-8-0 tender engines	3000–3999
All 0-6-0 tender engines	4000–5999
All electric locomotives	6000–6999
All 2-6-2, 4-4-2, 2-4-2, 0-4-4, and 4-4-4 tank engines	7000-7999
All 0-4-0, 0-4-2, 0-6-0 tank engines and diesel shunters	8000–8999
All other tank engines	9000-9999

Tender engines were numbered below 6000 and tank engines above 7000 apart from the solitary 4-6-4 tender locomotive which retained its original number 10000.

A 'breakdown' of numbers 1-999 illustrates how the scheme was carried out:

New No.	Class
1-34	A4
35-112	A3
113-	A1
500-	A2
800-983	V2

As no new 'A4' or 'A3' locomotives were to be built, Nos. 1-112 were used consecutively and then gaps were left in the 'A1' and 'A2' series for future additions. The final factor in deciding which number a locomotive would carry would be its building date, and so there would be almost a 'history' of any locomotive in its number.

The purists will also notice that there is a connection between the driving wheel diameters of the above group of locomotives and their numbers - the 'A1', 'A3' and 'A4' class have 6 ft 8 in. driving wheels, the 'A2' and 'V2' classes have 6 ft 2 in. driving wheels.

All very orderly, methodical and neat, but Thompson overlooked the physical problem of carrying out the renumbering.

The locomotives and the painters have to be available in the right place and at the right time, and although the manpower shortage was not quite as bad as it had been, providing sufficient painters to carry out the task in as short a time as possible was quite a headache.

As an example of what was involved, take a locomotive at random, say No. 2543. Under the new scheme it was due to become No. 44 so at the time that 2543 was renumbered, the locomotive receiving 2543 was renumbered; the locomotive receiving 2543 - a 'D16' - had to be available to have its new number allocated and the locomotive from which number 44 was to be removed had also to be available. If two locomotives were allowed to run carrying the same number, one can imagine the complications that might arise in the Accountant's Department!

The difficulties of organization were such that many locomotives carried temporary or 'interim' numbers before their final numbers were painted. Still, it's an ill wind and no doubt the staffs of the various paint shops involved welcomed the overtime.

The planning and organization that went into the scheme reflects great credit on those of Thompson's staff directly responsible for it and it must have been annoying to see the building date idea completely upset when it was decided that 'A4' Pacific *Sir Ronald Matthews* should be allocated number 1. The locomotive, built in March 1938 was originally named *Gargeney* and was renamed *Sir Ronald Matthews* after the chairman of the LNER in March 1939. Under Thompson's proposals it should have been numbered 609, but number 1 it became and set the precedent, the courtesy was extended to the locomotives bearing the names of Sir Murrough Wilson, Deputy Chairman, Andrew K. McCosh, Chairman of the Locomotive Committee, and so on to Supreme Commander of the Allied Forces, Dwight D. Eisenhower.

A Thompson coach - easily identifiable by the cross corridors and white Triplex lavatory windows.

British Railways

First class carriage No. 1531, the prototype for post-war LNER corridor stock.

British Railways

As it would have been impractical to have 'A4' Pacifics numbered amongst the 'A1s' and 'A3s', the 'A4s' were allocated numbers 1-34 inclusive and chronology went by the board (or should it be Board?)

Following all the complications and anomalies, the scheme was eventually completed, but it was short-lived. Under State ownership, the locomotives were again renumbered, but the nationalisation scheme was simpler in execution than had been Thompson's: 60000 being added to the number of each former LNER locomotive. Thus, some of them carried four numbers within the short space of five years. (Readers wishing to have full details of the renumbering scheme should refer to the masterly exposition that will be found in Part 1 of *Locomotives of the LNER* (RCTS 1963).)

Carriage & Wagon Work

Thompson's activities in the sphere of carriage and wagon design during his time as chief mechanical engineer were somewhat restricted by the war. The opportunities to break new ground were few and far between, but he took every advantage of those that were presented.

He was a regular visitor to Shildon works throughout the war and he continued to encourage the works manager, T.H.W. Cruddas, to improve wagon design. Thompson was particularly concerned with the elimination of timber from all stages of wagon construction, as it was in such short supply. With Cruddas he would design wagons on the shop floor and the drawing office staff at Stooperdale would eventually be informed and asked to prepare the necessary drawings. This method of working occasionally led to friction, but it was Thompson's aim to save time in production design, to eliminate waste and, as the wagon bodies were fabricated, to avoid the use of foundry capacity, and here again is a reminder of the demands placed on the LNER by the war. A large part of Shildon works was devoted to the manufacture of Oerlikon guns and, as the works was considered to be situated where enemy bombing was unlikely to be prevalent, large capacity drop forging stamps and upset forging machines were installed, depriving the company of a valuable wagon construction and repair service.

The introduction by Cruddas of the all-steel fabricated axle-box was an example of Thompson's ability, not only to cope with the abnormal conditions imposed upon him, but to turn these conditions to advantage. Despite the pressure he gave Cruddas every facility for the production of the axle-boxes, and then he insisted that the design - which was entirely Cruddas's - must be patented to protect both its designer and the LNER. This type of axle-box was produced in large numbers and was no doubt the right type at the time, but it was superseded by another design after Nationalisation.

In addition to the above, Thompson would occasionally carry out inspections on private owner's wagons, accompanied by Frank Day, his chief carriage & wagon draughtsman, and he was responsible for the repair and maintenance of the 'Warflats' and 'Warwells' supplied by the War Department for military use, both at home and overseas.

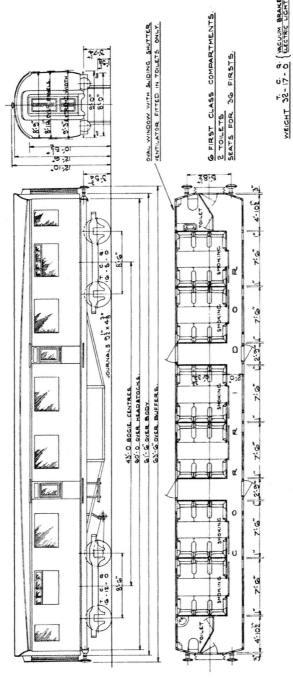

CORRIDOR FIRST

BUILT AT DONCASTER 1945

OVAL WINDOW WITH SLIDING SHUTTER
VENTILATOR FITTED IN TOILETS ONLY.

6 FIRST CLASS COMPARTMENTS.
2 TOILETS
SEATS FOR 36 FIRSTS.

T. C. 9. (VACUUM BRAKE.
WEIGHT 32-17-0 (ELECTRIC LIGHT.
WELDED UNDERFRAME.

43'-0 BOGIE CENTRES.
60'-0 OVER HEADSTOCKS.
61'-6 OVER BODY.
63'-6 OVER BUFFERS.

JOURNALS 5½"×48"

T. C. 9.
9'-6"-0

T. C. 9.
9'-6"-0

T. C. 9.
9'-12'-0

8'-6"

8'-6"

8'-6"

3'-6"
8'-1 LEFT

9'-5" LATERAL WIDTH.

8'-6"

8'-9"

9'-0"

10'-6"

12'-0"

But Thompson was not completely preoccupied with wagon work - he was also concerned about passenger comfort and introduced several modifications to coaching stock in an attempt to improve the lot of the traveller. He also sent Mr A.F. Cooper, then a technical assistant, to investigate conditions on London suburban services.

Notable amongst the modifications introduced were bucket seats, a bogie to replace the Gresley bogie and a heater based on a former North Eastern design. Unfortunately, in using both modified bogies and heaters, Thompson ran up against the vested interests of some of the Directors to such an extent that he was ordered to remove his version of the Gresley-Spencer-Moulton bogies from main line stock and use them on secondary stock.

The Stills heater was a device to which the LNER seemed eternally wedded and for efficient functioning it relied upon a wooden rod throughout its length acting as a thermostat. This used to char and become ineffective, so Thompson began to replace the Stills heaters with the North Eastern type mentioned above. In practice these were no more successful than the Stills type, being wasteful both of heat and materials. Thompson specified heavy gauge copper tubing, as one of this type of heater exploded during his North Eastern days and he was anxious to avoid a repetition.

One interesting departure from routine during the grim days of the war was the provision of an armour-plated carriage for General Dwight D. Eisenhower. A detachment of American troops was stationed at Doncaster works on the site of the burned out carriage shops and the LNER was approached to provide a special coach for the General's use. A sleeping car was used, several berths stripped out and it was fitted with living and working quarters. It was armour plated throughout and the General used it extensively in this country. When not in use it was usually located at Windsor, but always returned to Doncaster for overhaul and maintenance. A.H. Peppercorn was in charge of the project in close consultation with Thompson and Major Bingham of the US Army. This coach is now in a museum in Philadelphia.

But if Thompson is to be remembered as a carriage designer - and this is most unlikely - his name will be linked with the so-called 'Newton Coach'. This type of coach was introduced at the instigation of the CGM Sir Charles Newton and was precipitated by a fire that occurred on a north-bound train near Claypole. A group of boys was returning to Ampleforth College and amused themselves on the journey by flicking about lighted matches. The inevitable happened, a match lodged behind the trim in one of the coaches and in no time at all the end of the coach was ablaze. The fire spread rapidly and before it was brought under control five boys died, including the son of the Belgian Prime Minister M. Spaak, then in exile in England. Apart from the obviously inflammable nature of the materials used in construction, the design of the coach was criticised. It was argued that if cross-corridors with doors had been used instead of doors at the extreme ends of each coach, the loss of life might possibly have been avoided. Apart from this, it seems likely that the Board was anxious to alter the style of the coaches and to get away from wooden panelling and the practical difficulties of forming the curved ends of coaches.

Thompson followed Sir Charles Newton's suggestion and introduced a type of coach that had cross-corridors. It also had bucket seats and the distinguishing

'N7/1' class 0-6-2T No. 868 at Bishops Stortford shed in the 1930s. This locomotive was rebuilt into an 'N7/5' by Thompson in 1944. *Rail Archive Stephenson*

'N7/5' class 0-6-2T No. 69671 leaves Bethnal Green with a down Enfield train on 28th February, 1959. The 'N7/5s' had round-topped boilers and short travel valves. *R.C. Riley*

feature of elliptical lavatory windows glazed with white Triplex glass. He paid special attention to the nature of the materials used in construction and Lady Matthews acted as décor advisor.

The 'Newton Coach' was not, however, particularly successful, although it is generally considered to be the only worthwhile project that was undertaken in the Carriage Department during Thompson's years in office.

Conclusion

Thompson's major contributions to locomotive design have been reviewed in the foregoing pages - all that remains is to consider comparatively minor contributions.

Although Thompson devoted a large amount of his time and energy to modifications of some of Gresley's locomotives, he did very little to the Pacifics, of which he inherited a total of 114 engines, 'A1s', 'A3s' and 'A4s' all, of course, of Gresley design. It would be easy to theorise on this: lack of interest, fear of adverse criticism - both most unlikely - difficulties with the Locomotive Committee and so on, but Thompson was quite satisfied to keep this stud of fine locomotives in running order, and include them in his standardization plans. Apart from the *Great Northern* rebuild and the removal of the valances from the 'A4s' (and the 'W1' 4-6-4 locomotive, a much underrated machine, but that's another story), modifications to the Pacifics were carried out with a view to keeping them running at maximum efficiency. These modifications included the changing of some of the regulator valves from double beat to single seat balance type, an increase in cut-off from 65 to 75 per cent, in full forward gear, an increase in valve travel from $5\frac{5}{8}$ in. to $6\frac{5}{8}$ in., and were carried out as and when the valve gear required renewal.

The alterations were intended to overcome starting difficulties experienced with exceptionally heavy trains. The Pacifics were high powered locomotives, the 'A4s' particularly so, and, under wartime conditions, were called upon to perform tasks of haulage in excess of the designer's intentions. That they responded so well to the extra burden imposed upon them was a tribute to the excellence of the design, but they did have problems when coping with heavy loads from rest - these Thompson overcame with the modifications outlined above.

In an attempt to reduce the load imposed on the inside big-end bearing, Thompson proposed to fit liners to the middle cylinder, reducing its diameter to 17 in. He was authorized to carry out the work initially on six 'A4s', but there were delays and it was not done until after he had retired. Five of the six were fitted with middle cylinder liners during the latter part of 1947 and the work was then discontinued.

Other minor locomotive work that was carried out varied from the reboilering of former NER 4-6-2 tank engines to the introduction of a diesel-electric shunter in 1945 and is shown in *Appendix One*.

One of Thompson's more spectacular and less effective modifications was that carried out to Ivatt 4-4-0 locomotive No. 4075. It was turned out from

Ex-NER Raven 'A7' class 4-6-2T No. 1181 at West Hartlepool shed.

Colling Turner/Rail Archive Stephenson

'A7/1' class 4-6-2T No. 69771 ex-works in June 1948 at Darlington. The 'A7/1' class was rebuilt by Thompson from the Raven 'A7' and incorporated the 4 ft 9 in. 63B boiler.

E.V. Fry/Rail Archive Stephenson

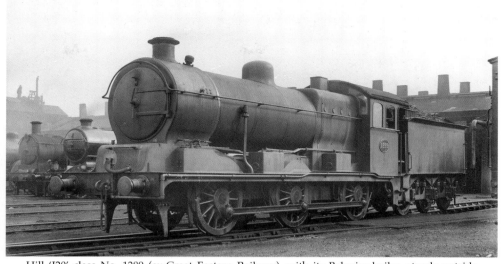

Hill 'J20' class No. 1289 (ex-Great Eastern Railway), with its Belpaire boiler, stands outside Stratford shed on 22nd September, 1923.   *W. Beckerlegge/Rail Archive Stephenson*

Thompson turned his attention to the 'J20' class in 1943 and fitted round-topped boilers. 'J20/1' class No. 64690 passes Kensington (Olympia) with a transfer goods from the Eastern Region to the Southern on 8th September, 1951.   *C.R.L. Coles/Rail Archive Stephenson*

Gresley 'O2' class 2-8-0 No. 3485 on shed at Doncaster on 1st May, 1937. This locomotive was rebuilt as a class 'O2/4' in August 1959.   *T.G. Hepburn/Rail Archive Stephenson*

The first conversions to class 'O2/4' took place in October 1943. No. 63975 passes through Worksop on 18th July, 1963. It was not converted until July 1962 which meant that it saw little over a year in service as an 'O2/4'. The rebuild saw the engines fitted with side cab windows and a 100A boiler.   *Rail Archive Stephenson*

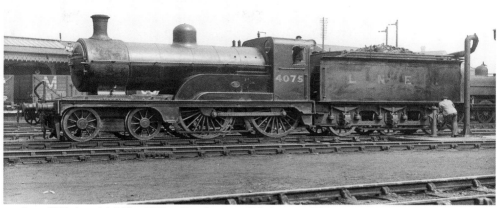

Ivatt 'D3' class 4-4-0 No. 4075 at Grantham on 10th August, 1938.
T.G. Hepburn/Rail Archive Stepehenson

No. 4075 was fitted with a two-window cab in 1944 for use hauling officers' special trains. The locomotive is seen here carrying its BR number, 62000, at Retford on 29th October, 1950.
W.S. Garth/Rail Archive Stephenson

Two Gresley 'B17' 4-6-0s, Nos. 2858 and 2870, were fitted with streamlined casing at Doncaster in 1937 for the use on the 'East Anglian' between Norwich and Liverpool Street. These two engines were re-classified 'B17/5'. No. 2870 *City of London* is seen at Grantham while on a running-in turn from Doncaster on 21st September, 1937. In 1941 the side skirting over the wheels was removed to allow easier access, as it was on the streamlined 'A4' class Pacifics (*see photographs opposite*), both engines being de-streamlined in April 1951. Nos. 2859 and 2870 were amongst the engines of the 'B17' class rebuilt with the 100A boiler and reclassified 'B17/6'. Although No. 2859 *East Anglian* received its 100A boiler in April 1949 it was not officially reclassified 'B17/6' until the streamlining had been removed. No. 2870 received its 100A boiler when de-streamlining took place.   *T.G. Hepburn/Rail Archive Stephenson*

In October 1943 Edward Thompson had two 'B17' class 4-6-0s, Nos. 2822 *Alnwick Castle* and 2864 *Liverpool*, which originally carried diagram 100 boilers, fitted with diagram 100A boilers. They retained their three-cylinder layout, unlike the 'B2' class (*see page 93*). By 1958 a total of 57 engines had been rebuilt in this manner. From December 1946 these locomotives were classified as 'B17/6s'. Thompson's locomotive renumbering scheme of 1946 saw *Liverpool* become No. 1664, this portrait shows it at Grantham shed on 6th October 1947.

T.G. Hepburn/Rail Archive Stephenson

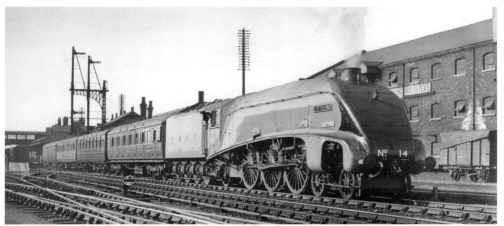

'A4' class No. 14 *Silver Link* powers away from Grantham with an up train on 30th August, 1946. This locomotive was one of five that became 'A4/1s' with inside cylinders lined up to 17 inches. The conversion was effected in August 1947 but was reversed in June 1949.

T.G. Hepburn/Rail Archive Stephenson

No. 3 *Andrew K. McCosh* emerges from Hadley Woood North tunnel with the up 'Flying Scotsman' in 1947. In June of that year it became the first 'A4' to be converted to an 'A4/1' and reverted to a standard 'A4' in June 1954.   *F.R. Hebron/Rail Archive Stephenson*

Doncaster in September 1944, with a new double-window cab, and, to quote the RCTS, a 'plethora of polished brass and copper fittings'.

The object of this exercise was to provide a locomotive of high route availability for the purpose of hauling Directors' and Officers' saloons and for some little time it was allocated number 1, but this was removed and it became 2000, the start of the 4-4-0 numbers under Thompson's renumbering scheme.

In addition to the brass and copper fittings, the locomotive was painted green and had the LNER crest handpainted on the tender side sheets. As far as can be ascertained, only four such crests were ever painted, two on No. 4472 *Flying Scotsman* when it was exhibited at Wembley in 1924 and two on the 4-4-0. When the locomotive was scrapped in 1951, the portions of the tender side sheets carrying the crests were cut out and framed. One was in the possession of Mr H. Clarkson of York and the other was acquired - appropriately enough - by J.F. Harrison.

This particular extravagance was not altogether successful. The engine was reboilered and overhauled in addition to being repainted, but it had a relatively short life. It spent long periods between Officers' Specials in store at Doncaster, a state of affairs that no doubt troubled the accountants, until it was eventually put into normal service whence it was withdrawn in October 1951.

'J45' 0-6-0 diesel-electric shunter - later classified 'DES 1' - No. 8002 at March shed in May 1948. Four locomotives of this type were built at Doncaster from 1944 to 1945, all were withdrawn in 1967.   *E.V. Fry/Rail Archive Stephenson*

Chapter Eight

Retirement 1946-1954

Thompson's five years as chief mechanical engineer of the LNER ended on 30th June, 1946 - five days after his 65th birthday - when he retired from the company's service.

To a great extent, the work that he had done and the contributions that he had made before his appointment as chief mechanical engineer were eclipsed by his years in office. The *LNER Magazine* for July 1946 made the following observation:

> Short as his term in office has been, Mr Thompson has left his mark on the locomotive history of the company and it is in that assurance that he is able to seek his well earned retirement.

The *Railway Gazette* of 21st June, 1946 contained a generous tribute in the course of which it reviewed Thompson's career noting that he had worked for four of the pre-Grouping companies and ended,

> It is already evident that in every way these medium powered engines [the 'B1s'] are proving very successful and we venture to predict an equal success for his fine new Pacifics one of which has just been named after him. Mr Thompson thus takes into retirement a very gracious tribute from the company that he has served with such energy.

The same edition noted the appointment of A.H. Peppercorn to succeed Thompson.

There was, of course, the usual round of ceremonies and presentations consequent upon the retirement of a senior official; these included a cheque for £120, an antique round dining table and chair, and a case of Dunhill pipes and Thompson gave a dinner party for his mechanical engineers, presenting each of them with a silver St Christopher medallion as a momento of the time that they had worked together. But as pleasant as these occasions were, the acknowledgement that pleased Thompson most, although he was reluctant to admit it, was the naming of 'Pacific' No. 500 *Edward Thompson*. This was done at the instigation and insistence of Sir Ronald Matthews and Andrew K. McCosh, both staunch supporters of Thompson's aims and policies. Some of the measure of his reaction to this gesture by the company can be gauged when he remarked afterwards that he felt that his wife would have been delighted.

Although Thompson did not look forward to his retirement, he set about making the best of it in characteristic fashion. He moved from Doncaster to a house that he had bought in Westgate-on-Sea and settled down to adjust to his new life. He sold his Standard 20 and hoped to replace it with a Wolseley 8, but deliveries were difficult and he eventually bought a Ford 'Anglia'. Never a very enthusiastic motorist, he used the car for local journeys and travelled longer distances by train, which was greatly to the relief of his friends as driving was not one of Thompson's strong points!

He occupied his time with golf, carpentry, watching shipping movements in the Channel, and frequent visits to Maurice and Lilian Hall at Brymbo. He had a lifelong interest in carpentry and had a workshop in his house at Westgate. The tools he used

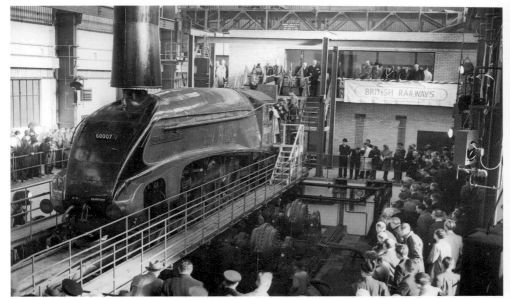

Official opening of the locomotive test plant at Rugby in 1948. The opening ceremony was performed by Rt Hon. Alfred Barnes, Minister of Transport in the Attlee Labour Government. Thompson was included on the VIP list along with as many pre-Nationalisation chief officers as were able to attend. The irony was that Gresley had advocated the test plant for several years before his death but did not live to see it come to fruition: the consolation was that 'A4' No. 60007 *Sir Nigel Gresley* was the first locomotive to be tested. *Author's Collection*

Rugby locomotive test plant - close up of the dynamometers. *Author's Collection*

were the traditional carpenters' tools - he eschewed the use of power-driven equipment. The furniture that he made has to be seen and handled to appreciate the craftsmanship. The miniature grandfather clock is particularly interesting as the case was made to accommodate a mantel clock and bears the legend 'Edward Thompson 1947'.

His interest in ships and shipping was such that Maurice and Lilian Hall invariably gave him a copy of *Jane's All the World's Ships* at Christmas and he was happy to travel to Dover and watch a great variety of shipping moving up and down the Straits. When asked what he would like to have been had he not devoted his life to railway work, Thompson unhesitatingly answered 'Admiral of the Fleet'. Perhaps he inherited his love of the sea from his great-great-grandfather.

Cricket also occupied much of his time and he was a frequent visitor to Lord's. He had been an MCC member for many years and when Maurice and Lilian Hall's son Tom was old enough, Thompson proposed him for MCC membership. Tom Hall showed great promise as a schoolboy cricketer and he was encouraged by Thompson who derived great pleasure from his progress. After an excellent cricketing career at Uppingham - he was team captain in 1948 - Tom Hall served an apprenticeship at Derby works under H.G. Ivatt and played for Derbyshire as an amateur. Thompson would endeavour to watch the county games in which Tom was playing and insisted on being taken from Brymbo to Leicester during his last illness and shortly before his death.

Thompson was very fond of the Hall's children and, as well as being delighted with Tom's cricketing progress, he was equally delighted when Wendy Hall married Major Robin Stratford-Tuke, grandson of Thompson's sister Margaret. After a successful Army career, Major Stratford-Tuke became Deputy Governor of Wandsworth Prison.

During his retirement, Thompson spent a great deal of his time with Maurice and Lilian Hall, who were then living in Brymbo. Maurice Hall was with the Brymbo Steel Company and through him Thompson maintained an interest in the affairs of industry. They usually went on holiday together and travelled extensively in Europe. Thompson also kept in touch with the railway world and visited Doncaster on several occasions. In 1948 he was invited to the opening of the locomotive testing plant at Rugby, a project that owed its origins to Sir Nigel Gresley, who had been very impressed with the work carried out at the SNCF testing plant at Vitry. For some years before his death, Gresley had advocated the establishment of a similar plant in this country as a joint enterprise of the four railway companies and work was started in 1937, but the 1939-45 war caused the project to be shelved and Gresley died without seeing the fulfilment of his plans. Thus, when the Rugby plant was completed and opened under British Railways in 1948 by the Rt Hon. Alfred Barnes, then Minister of Transport, former CME's of the four companies were invited, along with representatives of the SNCF. Appropriately, the first locomotive to be demonstrated at the plant was former LNER 'A4' Pacific *Sir Nigel Gresley*.

In 1949, Thompson's nephew, Conrad Powell-Johnstone, returned to the United Kingdom after 28 years in India with Shell Oil. His return coincided with difficulties that Thompson was experiencing in his domestic arrangements so he moved out of his house and his nephew took over. Thompson then moved into furnished rooms in Westgate with some arrangement with the owner over his meals. This had obvious disadvantages, but Thompson was never a businessman, relying upon Maurice Hall to look after his affairs. Thompson's lack of acumen led him into the unfortunate arrangements outlined and into an unhappy and unsettled phase of his retirement.

From then on, his visits to Brymbo became more frequent and prolonged. His friendship with the Halls had lasted over 13 years and he was turning to them more and more. They in their turn were pleased to welcome him to their home, but he did not take up permanent residence with them and maintained his rooms in Westgate.

And so the pattern continued - golf, carpentry, cricket and holidays abroad until early in 1954 when Thompson's health began to deteriorate. He complained of pains in his chest and left arm and was eventually persuaded by Lilian Hall to visit her family doctor, who suggested that Thompson should be seen by cardiologist Sir John Parkinson. This was arranged and a threatened coronary thrombosis was diagnosed, Sir John giving instructions that he was to be kept closely informed of Thompson's progress and contacted immediately should his condition worsen.

Thompson insisted on being taken to Leicester to see Tom Hall play against the county for Derbyshire. Maurice Hall recalled how he doubted the wisdom of his decision to take Thompson and wondered at one stage during the return journey, whether or not Thompson would reach Brymbo alive.

On 14th July, 1954, Thompson expressed a wish to walk to his local post-box to post some letters and set off, accompanied by Lilian Hall. On the way, however, he experienced severe pain in his chest and had to return to the house. Mrs Hall was very alarmed by his condition, and called in their family doctor, who immediately arranged for Sir John Parkinson to be informed and if possible to see Thompson on the following day. Next morning, however, the Hall's housekeeper was unable to rouse him - he had died during the night.

During his lifetime, particularly in his later working life, Thompson had to attend funerals, occasions that he always found depressing. He said several times that he did not want obsequies or mourning when he died and, in fact, left express wishes in his will to the effect that he was to be cremated, to have a short service according to the rites of the Established Church, and that there should be neither friends nor relatives present. These wishes were faithfully carried out and his body was cremated in Wrexham on 17th July, 1954.

His obituary in *The Times* of 16th July, 1954 occupied 22 lines and the private announcement, also in *The Times*, stated quite clearly that the cremation was private and that he was survived by his sister Katherine and nephews, great nephews and one niece. The 23rd July, 1954 edition of the *Railway Gazette* carried an obituary that contained much of the biographical detail that had been published when he was appointed.

Even in death, Thompson was not without his critics. Correspondence published in the Journal of the Stephenson Locomotive Society Vol. XLV 524, page 90 uses the fact that there was no one at his funeral as an illustration of his unpopularity The writer of this observation, in common with many other writers of parallel observations, failed to do his homework and thus does Thompson yet another injustice. If this book redresses the balance, or in some way contributes to a greater understanding of Thompson the man and what he was trying to achieve, then the effort involved will have been worthwhile.

Chapter Nine

The Final Analysis

If Edward Thompson is to be judged, by what standards is the judgement to be made? Is Bulleid judged on his 'Leader', Churchward and Raven on their Pacifics – all notable failures?

For too long, Thompson's less successful locomotive designs have been stressed, whilst his successful contributions have been merely acknowledged in passing. This is hardly an objective assessment, but it has the dubious quality of popular appeal and the ears of so-called enthusiasts have been inclined to the voices of those who have sought to discredit him.

Reference has already been made of some of the derisory comments that have been made about Thompson. Taking one at random, 'especially as Thompson was determined to rid the LNER of Gresley'. Let the facts speak for themselves: of the locomotive work carried out whilst Thompson was chief mechanical engineer, 20 Gresley engines were rebuilt and four more modified from Gresley designs, 24 in all, a rather small proportion of the total number of locomotives built to Thompson's designs. Furthermore, as pointed out in Chapter Seven he did not make radical changes to the Gresley Pacifics and he continued with the 'V2' building programme until 1943. Is this the work of a man determined to be rid of Gresley? Nor must it be forgotten that Thompson also rebuilt several locomotives of both Robinson and Raven designs, but as far as can be ascertained, no one has sprung to their defence or accused him of trying to deface the image of these two engineers.

Neither must the tremendous pressure placed on the LNER as a result of World War II - and *ipso facto* Thompson - be overlooked.

In 1939, the company had 172,000 employees, many of whom left to join the Services immediately after war was declared. This loss was, to a certain extent, offset by the direction of men and women into the company's service, but these 'pressed' employees, although making a splendid effort, did not have the railway tradition that meant so much to pre-war efficiency.

Furthermore, many of the older, skilled men were diverted from locomotive work to the production of armaments and their skills were lost, as indeed were the plant and equipment upon which they exercised these skills.

Repair and building space was at a premium, some part of each of the LNER's main works being given over to war work. To quote two instances, Dukinfield works concentrated on the manufacture of 6 in. shells and cartridge cases and York carriage and wagon works made naval dinghies and parts for gliders.

Military requirements, such as the large scale movements of troops and equipment, necessitated the construction of extra lines and connecting spurs and sidings. Special lines were also laid to facilitate the movement of munitions workers and in order to meet the needs of one factory near Harrogate, a circular section of track 6½ miles long was laid and 18,000 workers were moved every 24 hours.

Coal traffic was high on the list of priorities and there was an increased demand for this vital commodity. The closure of shipping routes meant that the burden of moving coal from the North East was placed on the LNER. Locomotives and rolling stock had to be found and, equally important, paths for the coal trains had to be provided. This was no easy task when one considers the other pressing demands for paths for troop trains, food trains, and evacuation trains as well as the normal day-to-day workings.

Another side effect of the increased demand for coal was that the LNER could no longer be selective in the type of coal used by its locomotives. Anything burnable was used and as a result the efficiency of the locomotives was impaired.

Then there was ordinary traffic - if the adjective can be used to describe rail travel during the war. The civilian population was on the move for a variety of reasons: moving away from danger areas, directed workers snatching weekends with their families and service personnel travelling to and from well-earned leaves. Transport had to be provided for them and at a time when passenger services had been drastically reduced to accommodate the essential trains already mentioned. Although statistics can be manipulated to prove a particular point, the following figures tell their own story.

In 1938, 141,000 tickets were issued at Grantham station; by 1942 this had risen to 315,000 and by 1945 to 411,000, and on one memorable day ticket sales at King's Cross were worth £20,000. In considering these figures it is well to bear in mind that they represent tickets sold and do not take into account tickets collected.

This outcome of this unprecedented demand was that trains made up of 18 bogies were commonplace, they were loaded to capacity and when, as often happened, passengers were left behind, relief trains were provided if this was humanly possible.

Having outlined, albeit briefly, the claims made upon the organization, upon the staff and upon the equipment, perhaps the reader can imagine the pressures to which the motive power depots and the workshops were subjected. On top of it all was the ever-present hazard of air raids, blackout conditions to cope with and extraneous duties such as fire watching to be done. That Thompson achieved all that he did was quite remarkable. His was the responsibility for maintaining the existing stock of locomotives, carriages and wagons at as high a level of performance as possible, of providing replacements and of planning ahead for a return to peacetime conditions. He was far too busy to sit at his desk, surrounded by acolytes, 'determined to rid the LNER of Gresley'.

Thompson's policy and efforts must be seen as a whole and in context and must not be condemned on the strength of his three-cylinder designs, which were not as successful as were Gresley's. From the rebuild of 'P2' *Thane of Fife*, to the entry into service of the last of his 'A2/3s', *Herringbone*, Thompson was responsible for 26 Pacifics. They were not revolutionary, they reflected his innate conservatism, but they pointed the way towards Peppercorn's 'A2s' and hence the 'A1s'.

Had Thompson been able to overcome his antipathy to unequal length connecting rods and had he been psychologically capable of redesigning the front end layout of his Pacifics, his successor would have had little to do in the way of 4-6-2 locomotive development. 'Freddie' Harrison disagreed with this premise and wrote,

> I was Peppercorn's assistant and know that both the 'A1s' and the 'A2s' were designed having a Gresley background, in other words a continuation of what we believed HNG would have come to - they were in our view logical successors to the Gresley high boiler pressured Pacifics.

The Peppercorn 'A1s' are acknowledged to be amongst the best Pacifics ever to run in this country - not from the partisan viewpoint of the enthusiast, but from that of the railwayman who is concerned with getting a train from A to B as expeditiously as possible.

The success of Thompson's two-cylinder locomotives is surely beyond question and, with the possible exception of the 'L1', compares very favourably with contemporary two-cylinder designs.

Acknowledged authorities on railway matters have expressed opinions on the relationship between Gresley and Thompson and in almost every instance these opinions are detrimental to Thompson. Whilst most experienced railway writers are capable of presenting reasoned and balanced views on a wide variety of railway topics from locomotive performance to high level decisions, it seems that the name of Thompson, particularly in context with that of Gresley, causes an emotional disturbance.

The truth of the matter is that during his lifetime very people were close enough to Thompson to obtain his views on the antagonism that is supposed to have existed between him and his CME. Of those who were close to him, none has felt inclined to record what Thompson thought about the affair. It has, therefore, been left to people to speculate and because the voices of those solidly behind Gresley have speculated most and loudest this reputed antagonism has been distorted and perpetuated by Sir Nigel's champions. What has really been damaging to Thompson's reputation is that this 'feud', if such it was, has influenced people in their judgement and assessment of his work as an engineer. In fairness to all, however, it must be conceded that Thompson was partly to blame. As has been noted his conservative attitude towards life precluded him from having acquaintances. He had friends, a select few to whom he was loyal and in whom he inspired loyalty, and he had working colleagues, but the two groups rarely, if ever, overlapped.

In later years Gresley did not appreciate Thompson's approach to engineering problems and his interest in education. He - Gresley - had gone straight from Marlborough to the shop floor whereas Thompson had gone to Cambridge. It has been suggested that Gresley felt inferior to Thompson by virtue of the latter's university background and social connections. This point was hotly disputed by the 'Gresley lobby' a member of which wrote,

> Gresley would not have felt socially inferior to Thompson: he [Gresley] came from one of the oldest families in England, who when created baronets in 1611 were already of high social standing.

Apart from their differences in approach to professional problems the two had a different approach to life. Thompson was very correct in his dress, speech and manners and was very reserved - a private person. Gresley, on the other hand, was bluff, ebullient, gregarious, fond of his share of drink and, towards the end of his life, fond of living in the style of a country gentleman. They had different senses of values and, as the two men progressed, became older and set in their ways, it was almost inevitable that their personalities would clash.

In the course of collecting material for this book, I have interviewed and corresponded with several people who were very much involved in the high echelons of the LNER under both Gresley and Thompson. No-one has been prepared to state that Thompson was deliberately held in check or frustrated by

Peppercorn 'A2' class 4-6-2 No. 60539 *Bronzino* with the down 'Heart of Midlothian' on 20th August, 1960, six miles north of Northallerton. This was the last Peppercorn 'A2' Pacific to be built, introduced in 1947, it was fitted with a double blast pipe.   *Author's Collection*

Peppercorn 'K1' class 2-6-0 No. 62005 double-heads with BR/Sulzer type '2' Bo-Bo No D5160 on the Stephenson Locomotive Society's 'Three Dales Tour' as it enters Leyburn station on 20th May, 1967.   *N. Stead Collection*

Gresley, apart from the instance mentioned below but there is a view from some of them that Thompson did in fact intend to undo Gresley's work. There are instances of them having differences of opinion - who has not fallen out with the boss at some time? - and there is no doubt that there was a certain degree of tenseness between them. Despite his natural reserve, Thompson was an individualist just as much as was Gresley, and if he had a point to make it was made.

The only suggestions of an open clash came in the months before Gresley's death. He was obviously far from well at this time and yet he drove himself as hard as ever. His death was indirectly attributable to the fact that he insisted on attending a meeting of chief mechanical engineers when he ought to have taken things quietly. He was to chair his particular meeting and in his absence the chair would have been taken by Sir William Stanier. As Gresley had some important point that he wanted to raise, he deemed it politic to be present. In any case, he didn't want Stanier in the chair. It was, however, the 'last straw' - the strain was too much and he was taken ill and died a few weeks later.

Gresley presided at meetings of his mechanical engineers like the Prime Minister presiding over a Cabinet meeting - in some ways the analogy is quite apt - and he developed the habit of asking for Thompson's opinion, assuming that opinions were required, after everyone else had spoken, with 'Now, let's hear what Thompson has to say', or 'Well Thompson, and what do you think of the idea?' It was at one of these meetings that Gresley peremptorily dismissed Thompson's proposals for the rebuilding of a former GCR 4-6-0 referred to on page 35. Thompson took these slights very well, but he exercised restraint on more than one occasion.

There is evidence that Gresley and Thompson socialised occasionally and during the time that the Thompsons were living in Hurworth, Gresley spent a weekend with them. (Gresley's wife died in 1929 at the age of 54 and he never fully recovered from her death.) It was a pleasant enough occasion and, on leaving, Gresley insisted that Mrs Thompson should have some token of his appreciation of her hospitality. If she would arrange for her chauffeur to meet a certain train, there would be a parcel on it for her. This was done and on opening the parcel, it was found to contain a signed photograph of Gresley! Even he wasn't immune to conceit.

I started work on this book not because I was strongly pro-Thompson - I have no emotional involvement with the man or his machines - but because I was curious; curious about Thompson and about the way that he had been either roughly treated or ignored by the established authors. In this respect he was undoubtedly the architect of his misfortunes by virtue of his unapproachable manner. In the first edition I wrote, 'Indeed, if he were still alive, it is most unlikely that this book would have been written at this time'. In response to this comment and in a letter to me , E.S. Cox wrote, 'You say that if he had been alive the book would never have been written, but I have a feeling that he might have found it very agreeable in the manner in which you have presented him'.

Let Edward Thompson be remembered not only as the man who rebuilt some of the LNER's sacred cows and sent members of Gresley's staff into the wilderness, but also as the man who designed the 'B1', introduced the 'O1' and showed A.H. Peppercorn the way to the 'A1' and 'K1'. Let it also be remembered that he was somewhat introspective, saddened by the untimely death of his wife and by his lack of a family: remember that Edward Thompson was human.

Name

E. [monogram] Thompson

Born June 25: 1881
Ent.d Service Aug 1: 1906

Left N.E. and joined
G.N.Co Dec. 3rd 1911
Re-entd N.E. Co Nov 1st 1920

Transferred to Stratford Aug: 1st 1927.

Mechanical Engineer, Dton. Jan. 1st 1934
    "   "   Donc. " 1st 1938
C. M. E.   "

retired June 30/46.

Salary advanced to:-

£300 on Feb 1st 1909
 350 " Jany 1st 1911

York C.&W. Works Mangr
£1.400 on Nov 1st 1920

✻ Carr & Wagon Workshops Mangr
£1.580 on June 1st 1923
✻ Designation to be "Carriage & Wagon
Works Manager, North Eastern Area"
as per Cmt letter 5/7/11 of 24/6/24.

An extract from Edward Thompson's employment record.

Epilogue

I quote from the final section of an article written by Richard Hardy in issue No. 110 of the *Gresley Observer*:

If you choose to remember Edward Thompson for his work, judge him by his successes as you would Gresley. But I choose to remember him as a man of dignity, charm and kindness. He was not petty minded. He may have been obstinate at times but so was Gresley for they were powerful men and were none the worse for that. Thompson could fly into a rage, so they say and he was said to be difficult and unreasonable. His engineering ability has been questioned, maybe he was a better administrator than an engineer. But so were some of the great names of the past and there is no shame in that so long as they could pick their subordinates. It has been said that reports of inspectors and technical assistants in the running department about the performance of Thompson engines were influenced by fear of reprisal from the CME.

This could not be so. Headquarters inspectors and technical assistants reported to the Locomotive Running Superintendent. The likes of L.P. Parker wanted the truth and they got it. The report to the CME would be signed by the LRS who would accept total responsibility for what was said. There was no question of his staff being effectively criticised by high ranking officers from other departments and, if flack were to be taken, the LRS would take it and fight his corner. But LPP was nearly always right and could deal with a mere CME! They say that Gresley did not like that but Thompson did for he knew his man.

Five hard years, hellish wartime conditions, a good understanding of what was required for the present and the future, some good engines - some also rans too - a principled chief, a man of courage, remote perhaps but respected throughout his huge department which covered so many facets of engineering, respected by his superiors, not least by his Chairman, Sir Ronald Matthews. So now let Edward Thompson rest in peace for he did his job.

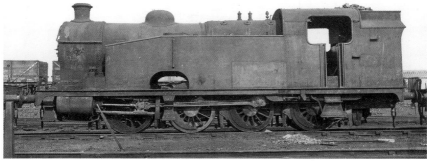

'Q1' class 0-8-0T No. 69936 at Frodingham on 6th July, 1958. Nos. 69935 and 69936 were the last two members of the class to be withdrawn in September 1959.

Author's Collection

Appendix One

Summary of Thompson's Locomotive Work

Class	Former class	Original Designer	Notes	Date introduced	Date extinct	Illustrated page No.
A1	A1	Gresley	Rebuild of 4470 - later reclassified A1/1 - Jan. 1948.	Sep. 1945	Nov. 1962	98
A2/2	P2	Gresley	Rebuild of P2 2-8-2, initially classified A.	Jan. 1943	Feb. 1962	59
A2/1	-	Gresley	Modification of V2 design.	Apr. 1944	Feb. 1961	70
A2/3	A2	Thompson	Introduced as A2, subsequently reclassified A2/3.	May 1946	Jun. 1965	112
A4/1	A4	Gresley	Classification introduced after Thompson's retirement applied to A4s with lined-up middle cylinders.	Jun. 1947	Sep. 1966	129
A7/1	A7	Raven	Rebuild with 4 ft 9 in. 63B diameter boiler.	Sep. 1943	Dec. 1967	124
B1	-	Thompson	Standard general utility type originally classified B.	Apr. 1943	Sep. 1967	49
B2	B17	Gresley	Rebuilt from B17 'Sandringham' class.	Aug. 1945	Dec. 1959	94
B3/3	B3/2	Robinson	Rebuild with two outside cylinders and Walschaert's valve gear.	Oct. 1945	Apr. 1949	62
B12/4	B12	Holden	Rebuilt with 5 ft 1½ in. dia. 25A boiler and round-topped firebox.	Jul. 1943	Nov. 1953	92
B16/3	B16/1	Raven	Rebuilt from Raven locomotive.	May 1944	Nov. 1964	76
B17/6	-	Gresley	Reboilering programme planned by Thompson.	Dec. 1946	Aug. 1960	128
D	D49/2	Gresley	Rebuilt with two inside cylinders from D49/2 class. Only one locomotive in the class.	Aug. 1942	Nov. 1952	88
D3	D3	Ivatt	Reboiled and overhauled: intended for use with Directors' Saloon. Only one locomotive.	Sep. 1944	Oct. 1951	127
J11	J11/3	Robinson	Rebuilds with long travel piston valves.	Jul. 1942	Oct. 1962	46
J20/1	J20	Hill	Reboilered with round-topped firebox.	Oct. 1943	Sep. 1962	125
J45	-	Thompson	Diesel electric shunter - subsequently classified DES1.	May 1945	1967	130
K1	K4	Gresley	Two-cylinder rebuild from K1, subsequently reclassified K1/1. Only one locomotive.	Dec. 1945	Jun. 1961	108
K5	K3/2	Gresley	Two-cylinder rebuild based on K3/2 – boiler pressure raised to 225 lb./sq. in. Only one locomotive.	Jun. 1945	Jun. 1960	90
L1	-	Thompson	First completely new post-war design MT tank engine.	May 1945	Dec. 1962	82
N7/5	N7/1	Gresley	Original N7/1 rebuilt with round-topped firebox.	May 1943	Sep. 1962	122
O1	O4	Robinson	Rebuilt from O4, new cylinders, 100A boiler.	Feb. 1944	Aug. 1965	68
O2/4	-	Gresley	Three-cylinder locomotives given 100A boilers.	Oct. 1943	Dec. 1963	126
O4/8	-	Robinson	Rebuilds with 100A boilers, carried out after Thompson's retirement.	Dec. 1946	Apr. 1966	64
Q1	-	Robinson	Tank locomotive rebuilt from Q4 tender locomotive sub-classes Q1/1 and Q1/2.	Jun. 1942	Sept. 1959	44

Appendix Two

Locomotive Trials

By the beginning of 1945, Thompson had been CME for nearly four years and he was called upon by the Chief General Manager to submit a report upon the economic effects of some of the changes that his locomotive policy had brought about. In order to assess relative fuel consumptions, trials were arranged and a member of Thompson's staff, G.A. Musgrave, was in charge. The locomotives involved were 'A2/2' No. 2003 (BR 60503) *Lord President*, 'A2/1' No. 3697 (BR 60508) *Duke of Rothesay*, 'A4' No. 2512 (BR 60017) *Silver Fox* and the trains were 10.30 am King's Cross-Leeds, returning at 7.30 am next day; the 12.40 am King's Cross-Grantham, returning at 3.17 pm. Although the timings were easy, the loads were heavy. Freight workings were also involved and consisted of fast runs to Peterborough from King's Cross and return.

The results of the first series were so poor - bad weather conditions and unfamiliarity of the crews with the Thompson engines were thought to be responsible - that the trials were re-run in the following spring. In these tests, the results were better and details of both series are shown below.

Engine	Date of Trial	lb. coal/mile		lb. coal/ton mile		Remarks
2003	Feb. 1945	70.8				
3697	Feb. 1945	69.0				Tests repeated for passenger
2512	Feb. 1945	52.3				workings only
2003	Feb. 1945	62.8				
3697	Feb. 1945	60.2				
		Pass.	Freight	Pass.	Freight	
2003	Apr./May	46.1	45.4	.084	.076	Substantial reduction probably
3697	Apr./May	43.3	41.4	.079	.076	due to crews having become
2512	Apr./May	40.5	45.2	.075	.072	familiar with engines.

Lessons may have been learned from these trials, but as there were certain basic differences between the locomotives involved one questions the value of the results - there was a difference in boiler pressure and coupled wheel diameter between the 'A2s' and the 'A4': the 'A2s' were fitted with rocking grates and hopper ash pans. It would seem, however, that one benefit that resulted was the removal of the steam reversing gear from No. 3697 and its demise - it never reappeared on any further LNER designs.

After having completed the trials outlined above No. 4470 *Great Northern* was tested against 'A4' Pacific No. 4466 *Sir Ralph Wedgwood*. The timings of the trains involved had been increased somewhat over those in the 'A2'/'A4' trials, but the loads were reduced. The overall result was a reduction in the coal consumption per mile, but an increase in the coal consumed per train ton mile.

Engine	Date of Trial	lb. coal/mile	lb. coal/ton mile	Remarks
4470	Nov. 1945	39.8	0.85	Double blast pipe and chimney
4466	Nov. 1945	39.9	0.86	Single blast pipe and chimney

There is no doubt that Thompson used the data collected from the above trials in finalising the designs for his 'A2' Pacifics introduced in 1946. It is not surprising, therefore, that the 'A2/3' prototype *Edward Thompson* also figured in trials. This time, however, the trials were held in the North Eastern section of the LNER and competition was provided by a 'V2' 2-6-2 locomotive.

Before dealing with this particular series of tests, it is worth mentioning that when the 'A2/3' prototype was given its proving run, it worked a train of 17 coaches and the dynamometer car on a Leeds-Newcastle-Leeds turn. The train entered Bramhope tunnel at the prescribed speed of 35 mph, developing almost 2,000 drawbar horsepower in the process. On that occasion, Thompson himself was on the train.

In the 'A2/3'-'V2' trials, the trains selected were the 9.45 am Newcastle-Leeds, the 1.50 pm Leeds-Newcastle, the 11.11 am Newcastle-Edinburgh, and the 5.25 pm Edinburgh-Newcastle, the loads being increased to just over 500 tons for test purposes. Unfortunately, the tests were dogged with variables from the start, not the least of these being poor quality coal and atrocious weather, and the results were virtually inconclusive. The only significant points that the official report mentioned were that the 'A2/3' blast-pipe and chimney arrangement was superior to that on the 'V2' and that the 'A2/3' had greater haulage capacity than the 'V2'.

1948 Inter-Regional Exchanges

These were held shortly after Nationalisation and lasted from April to September 1948. The object was to provide information from which a standard range of British Railways could be designed and Thompson was represented by 'B1s' Nos. 61292 *Oliver Bury*, 61163 and 61251, and by 'O1s' Nos. 63773 and 63789. The routes over which the engines operated, and the loads that were hauled, are shown below.

Mixed Traffic - 'B1s'

Region	Route	Load	Remarks
Scottish	Perth/Inverness	350 tons Perth/Aviemore	Assisted in rear Blair
		255 tons Aviemore/Inverness	Atholl-Dalnaspidal
Lond. Midland	St Pancras/Manchester		310 tons
Western	Bristol/Plymouth	420/450 tons	275 tons west of Newton Abbot
Eastern	Marylebone/Manchester		373 tons

Freight - 'O1s'

Region	Route	Load - Wagons Up	Load - Wagons Down
London Midland	Brent/Toton	68	84
Western	Acton/Severn Tunnel Jn	40-65	57-65
Eastern	Ferme Park/Peterborough	60	80
Western & Southern	Bristol/Eastleigh	60	60

A full analysis and assessment of the 1948 trials would be out of place here. In any case, Cecil J. Allen deals with the subject fully in his *The Locomotive Exchanges* (Ian Allan, 1949) but it must be stated that the five Thompson engines involved gave very good accounts of themselves. It would be pointless to quote a string of figures for, say, the 'B1s' showing performances throughout the tests unless figures for comparable locomotives were also quoted, but the following abbreviated table will give some indication of the way in which the 'B1s' and 'O1s' behaved under test conditions.

Mixed Traffic Engines

Regional Design	Type	Route	lb. coal/ train mile	lb. coal/ dbhp hr
Western	Hall	Western	46.91	4.11
		Eastern	46.75	3.84
Eastern	B1	Western	46.92	3.96
		Eastern	41.80	3.32
		London Midland	33.70	3.34
		Scottish	49.53	4.01
London Midland	5	Western	39.21	3.39
		Eastern	40.49	3.29
		London Midland	38.15	3.71
		Scottish	48.28	3.90
Southern	West Country	Western	52.97	4.28
		Eastern	50.29	3.90
		London Midland	43.44	3.80
		Scottish	63.24	3.77

Scottish routes included the severe climb to Druimuachadar and the Western routes from Newton Abbot included Dainton , Rattery and Hemerdon banks.

Freight Engines

Regional Design	Type	Route	lb. coal/ train mile	lb. coal/ dbhp hr
Western	28XX	Western	57.85	3.54
		Eastern	67.74	3.25
		Western, Southern	59.67	3.43
Eastern	O1	Western	56.70	3.37
		Eastern	62.46	3.25
		London Midland	74.54	3.31
		Western, Southern	62.17	3.63
London Midland	8F	Western	59.04	3.81
		Eastern	58.14	3.17
		London Midland	82.20	3.48
		Western, Southern	66.57	3.58
London Midland	WD 2-8-0	Western	66.65	4.02
		Eastern	63.89	3.56
		London Midland	79.04	3.55
		Western, Southern	71.84	4.11
London Midland	WD 2-10-0	Western	56.70	3.59
		Eastern	60.17	3.09
		London Midland	80.53	3.65
		Western, Southern	69.08	3.66

Appendix Three

Names, Numbers and Dates

Of the new locomotives built to Thompson's designs, comparatively few were named. Rebuilt locomotives that were originally named retained them, and for the purposes of this appendix no distinction is shown between new and rebuilt engines.

The policy behind the naming of the 'B1s' has already been mentioned. In April 1946 when No. 1040 (BR 61404) was put into traffic, Thompson suggested that it ought to be named 'Utility', but the Chief General Manager, Sir Charles Newton, did not approve of the idea. Thus, the last of the 'B1s' named after antelopes became *Roedeer* at his suggestion.

No. 61379 was named *Mayflower* in July 1951 to mark the visit to this country of the Pilgrim Fathers' Association of Boston, Massachusetts, USA, and worked a special train from King's Cross to Boston Lincolnshire immediately after the naming ceremony. Thereafter it was allocated to Immingham and carried commemorative plaques on the cab sides. It was the last of the 'B1s' to be named.

Apart from the'B1s', only the Pacifics were named. The 'A2/2s' rebuilt from the 'P2s' kept their original names, although *Thane of Fife* ran un-named for some time until the discarded front end of the 'P2' complete with nameplates was discovered on a scrapheap. The nameplates were recovered, restored and attached to No. 60505. *Wolf of Badenoch* also ran without nameplates for a while after rebuilding.

The 'A2/1s', which it will be remembered were developed from the Gresley 'V2s', ran nameless for a time until they were given Scottish names and the 'A2s', apart from No. 500 (BR 60500) *Edward Thompson,* were named in the LNER tradition, after racehorses.

Class	BR No.	Name	Built	W'drawn
A1	60113	Great Northern	9/1945	11/1962
A2/3	60500	Edward Thompson	5/1946	6/1963
A2/2	60501	Cock o' the North	9/1944	2/1960
	60502	Earl Marischal	6/1944	7/1961
	60503	Lord President	12/1944	11/1959
	60504	Mons Meg	11/1944	1/1961
	60505	Thane of Fife	1/1943	11/1959
	60506	Wolf of Badenoch	4/1944	4/1961
A2/1	60507	Highland Chieftain	5/1944	12/1960
	60508	Duke of Rothesay	6/1944	2/1961
	60509	Waverley	11/1944	8/1960
	60510	Robert the Bruce	1/1945	11/1960
A2/3	60511	Airborne	7/1946	11/1962
	60512	Steady Aim	8/1946	6/1965
	60513	Dante	8/1946	4/1963
	60514	Chamossaire	9/1946	12/1962
	60515	Sun Stream	10/1946	11/1962
	60516	Hycilla	11/1946	11/1962
	60517	Ocean Swell	11/1946	11/1962
	60518	Tehran	12/1946	11/1962
	60519	Honeyway	2/1947	12/1962
	60520	Owen Tudor	3/1947	6/1963
	60521	Watling Street	5/1947	11/1962
	60522	Straight Deal	6/1947	6/1965
	60523	Sun Castle	8/1947	6/1963
	60524	Herringbone	9/1947	2/1965

Class	BR No.	Name	Built	W'drawn
B1	61000	*Springbok*	12/1942	3/1962
	61001	*Eland*	6/1943	9/1963
	61002	*Impala*	9/1943	6/1967
	61003	*Gazelle*	11/1943	12/1965
	61004	*Oryx*	12/1943	12/1963
	61005	*Bongo*	2/1944	9/1962
	61006	*Blackbuck*	3/1944	9/1963
	61007	*Klipspringer*	4/1944	2/1964
	61008	*Kudu*	5/1944	12/1966
	61009	*Hartebeeste*	6/1944	9/1962
	61010	*Wildebeeste*	11/1946	11/1965
	61011	*Waterbuck*	11/1946	11/1962
	61012	*Puku*	11/1946	6/1967
	61013	*Topi*	12/1946	12/1966
	61014	*Oribi*	12/1946	12/1966
	61015	*Duiker*	1/1947	11/1962
	61016	*Inyala*	1/1947	10/1965
	61017	*Bushbuck*	2/1947	11/1966
	61018	*Gnu*	2/1947	11/1965
	61019	*Nilghai*	2/1947	3/1967
	61020	*Gemsbok*	2/1947	11/1962
	61021	*Reitbok*	3/1947	6/1967
	61022	*Sassaby*	3/1947	11/1966
	61023	*Hirola*	4/1947	10/1965
	61024	*Addax*	4/1947	5/1966
	61025	*Pallah*	4/1947	12/1962
	61026	*Ourebi*	4/1947	2/1966
	61027	*Madoqua*	5/1947	9/1962
	61028	*Umseke*	5/1947	10/1962
	61029	*Chamois*	6/1947	12/1966
	61030	*Nyala*	6/1947	9/1967
	61031	*Reebuck*	7/1947	11/1964
	61032	*Stembok*	8/1947	11/1966
	61033	*Dibatag*	8/1947	3/1963
	61034	*Chiru*	10/1947	12/1964
	61035	*Pronghorn*	10/1947	12/1966
	61036	*Ralph Assheton* (allocated *Korrigum*)*	11/1947	9/1962
	61037	*Jairou*	11/1947	5/1964
	61038	*Blacktail*	12/1947	5/1964
	61039	*Steinbok*	12/1947	6/1965
	61040	*Roedeer*	4/1946	7/1966
	61189	*Sir William Gray*	5/1947	5/1967
	61215	*William Henton Carver*	7/1947	3/1965
	61221	*Sir Alexander Erskine Hill*	8/1947	3/1965
	61237	*Geoffrey H. Kitson*	9/1947	12/1966
	61238	*Leslie Runciman*	9/1947	2/1967
	61240	*Harry Hinchcliffe*	10/1947	12/1966
	61241	*Viscount Ridley*	10/1947	12/1962
	61242	*Alexander Reith Gray*	10/1947	7/1964
	61243	*Sir Harold Mitchell*	10/1947	5/1964
	61244	*Strang Steel*	10/1947	10/1965
	61245	*Murray of Elibank*	10/1947	7/1965
	61246	*Lord Balfour of Burleigh*	10/1947	12/1962
	61247	*Lord Burghley*	10/1947	6/1962
	61248	*Geoffrey Gibbs*	10/1947	11/1965
	61249	*Fitzherbert Wright*	10/1947	6/1964
	61250	*A. Harold Bibby*	10/1947	4/1966
	61251	*Oliver Bury*	11/1947	4/1964
	61379	*Mayflower*	6/1951	8/1962

* The nameplate *Korrigum* was cast but never carried.

'D' class 4-4-0 No. 62768 *The Morpeth* showing the accident damage sustained that led to its early withdrawal in November 1952.   *Author's Collection*

Class	BR No.	Name	Built	W'drawn
B2	61603	*Framlingham*	10/1946	9/1958
	61607	*Blickling*	5/1947	12/1959
	61614	*Castle Hedingham*	11/1946	6/1959
	61615	*Culford Hall*	4/1946	2/1959
	61616	*Falloden*	11/1945	9/1959
	61617	*Ford Castle*	12/1946	8/1958
	61632	*Belvoir Castle*	7/1946	2/1959
	61639	*Norwich City*	1/1946	5/1959
	61644	*Earlham Hall*	3/1949	11/1959
	61671	*Royal Sovereign*	6/1945	9/1958
B3/3	61497	*Earl Haig* (nameplate removed on rebuilding)	10/1943	4/1949
D	62768	*The Morpeth*	8/1942	11/1952
K1	61997	*MacCailin Mor*	12/1945	6/1961

'K1/1' class 2-6-0 No. 61997 *MacCailin Mor* with the 12.30 pm Mallaig-Fort William train between Lochailort and Glenfinnan in the summer of 1955.

W.J. Verden Anderson/Rail Archive Stephenson

Appendix Four

Preservation

The two examples of Thompson's locomotive design that exist - both 'B1s' - are No. 61306, originally owned by the B1 Preservation Society and No. 61264 owned by the Thompson Locomotive Trust as previously mentioned. No. 61306 was saved from the scrap heap by the efforts of A.G. Priestley and Richard Hadingham who formed the B1 Preservation Society, subsequently changing the name to the B1 Locomotive Society Ltd and they were chairman and secretary/treasurer respectively.

Built by the North British Locomotive Co., the locomotive entered service in April 1948 and was withdrawn in September 1967. In the months prior to this date the enthusiasm of Messrs Priestley and Hadingham was largely responsible for raising the £3,000 required by British Rail for No. 61306. Following its final in-service run, with Mr Hadingham on the footplate, the engine returned to Normanton motive power depot and was handed over to the society. Thus instead of making the journey form Normanton to the scrapyard, the 'B1' was stored at Wakefield and was subjected to a certain amount of vandalism.

In the meantime, the Lakeside Railway Society had bought a Fairburn class '4' 2-6-4 for preservation at its Carnforth depot and this locomotive joined the 'B1' at Wakefield. At this point, the two societies co-operated and No. 61306 was taken to Carnforth in the company of the Fairburn tank No. 42085 on 1st May, 1968.

Preservation is one thing, restoration is another, and an inspection carried out by engineers from the Hunslet Engine Co. revealed that whilst the engine was in reasonable condition, it would cost an estimated £2,500 to restore it to running order and to paint it in LNER apple green livery (1968 prices). As funds were nearing exhaustion, what little was in the pot was used to prevent further deterioration. No. 61306 was kept under cover ensuring that the engine was protected from the ravages of both the weather and souvenir hunters and the society paid its share towards the running costs of Carnforth motive power depot.

'B1' class 4-6-0 No. 61306 in store before being overhauled at Carnforth and passed into preservation as No. 1306 *Mayflower* resplendent in apple green.   *Author's Collection*

'B1' class 4-6-0 No. 1306 on the turntable at Carnforth on 1st May, 1971 after being ceremonially named *Mayflower*.   *Author's Collection*

It was ever the ambition of Messrs Priestley and Hadingham to restore No. 61306 to working order, to paint it LNER green, to revert to its original number - 1306 - and to name it *Mayflower*. the name allocated to No. 61379 in July 1951. No. 61379 had been withdrawn in August 1962 so there was no question of there being two *Mayflower's* and with the help and support of the late Edgar Shone, the ambition was realised. On 1st May, 1971 - three years to the day that it entered Carnforth and with no small amount of flummery including a Post Office first day cover - No. 1306 was wheeled out resplendent in apple green and carrying *Mayflower* nameplates covered by a Union flag. A party of VIPs including Messrs Priestley and Hadingham and Peter Beet, the *supremo* of Carnforth, assembled on the turntable and, with due ceremony, Edgar Shone broke the flag and the 'B1' moved out into the country. All very well but the event had about it the dark inevitability of a Greek tragedy and after Edgar Shone withdrew his support the locomotive was taken over by Steamtown and did some main line work including taking part in the Shildon Cavalcade in September 1975. In 1978 it was sold and moved to the Great Central Railway and moved again in 1989, this time to Hull Dairycoates. In May 1991 it went to Wansford, on the Nene Valley Railway, where an overhaul was completed, and it still remains there today.

A correspondent writing in the *Railway Magazine* for November 1969 reported that 'K1' class locomotive No. 62005 was stored at Neville Hill depot, Leeds. Although this engine was built after Thompson's retirement and the class is listed as a Peppercorn development of Thompson's design, it can be argued therefore that the two 'B1s' are not the sole examples of Thompson's work still in existence.

No. 62005 ended its working life quietly on Teeside and was reported *en route* for the Hunsley Engine Co.'s Works on 1st January, 1969. The information then available suggested that its boiler was to be used on Lord Garnock's preserved 'K4' *The Great Marquess* which had failed an insurance test. This was not possible, however, and No. 62005 went to the North York Moors Railway. It has had a very busy and useful working life since being withdrawn in 1969 which is more than can be said for *The Great Marquess*.

Bibliography

The British Steam Locomotive 1825-1925 by E.L. Ahrons (Locomotive Publishing Co.)

Sir Vincent Raven and the North Eastern Railway by Peter Grafton (Oakwood Press)

Thompson and Peppercorn - Locomotive Engineers by Col H.C.B. Rogers (Ian Allan)

Locomotive Adventure by H. Holcroft (Ian Allan)

The Locomotive Exchanges by C.J. Allen (Ian Allan)

British Pacific Locomotives by C.J. Allen (Ian Allan)

Locomotive Panorama by E.S. Cox (Ian Allan)

LNER Steam by O.S. Nock (David & Charles)

Locomotives of the LNER, Standardization and Renumbering by O.S. Nock (LNER)

Four Thousand Miles on the Footplate by O.S. Nock (Ian Allan)

British Steam Locomotives at Work by O.S. Nock (Ian Allan)

Yeadon's Register of LNER Locomotives, Volume Six: Thompson B1 class by W.B. Yeadon (Irwell Press)

Locomotives of the LNER (RCTS)

Railway Gazette

LNER Magazine

Gresley Observer

Index

Armour-plated carriage (Eisenhower's), 121

Bailey, Capt. John, 10

Baister, Charles, 13, 16

Baister, S.L., 13

Banbury, Sir Frederick, 17

Beckett, Rupert E., 55

Beyer, Peacock & Co., 13, 14

Bond, R.C., 37

Brooks, Billy, 57

Bulleid, O.V.S., 7, 13, 37

Cambridge University, 10, 11

Carriage & Wagon work, 119 *et seq.*

Cockman, F.G., 6, 53, 113

Cox, E.S., 39 *et seq.*, 99, 139

Cruddas, T.H.W., 5, 27 *et seq.*, 119

Darlington works (and later NER HQ), 16, 26 *et seq.*, 53, 54, 71, 78

Directors' names on locomotives, 54, 55, 117

Doncaster works, 16, 17, 27, 33 *et seq.*, 39, 41, 69, 79, 97, 99, 109, 121, 130

Dukinfield works, 135

Dwight D. Eisenhower, 117, 121

Gateshead works (and first NER HQ), 13, 14, 54

Geddes, Eric, 17

General Strike, 22, 24

Glaze, C.W.L., 22, 23

Gould, C.G., 73, 75

Gorton works, 45, 61, 63

Great Central Railway, 19, 39, 78

Great Eastern Railway, 19, 23, 25, 81, 91, 99

Great Northern Railway, 16, 20, 39, 89, 97

Gresley, (Sir) H. Nigel, 5, 7, 11, 15 *et seq.*, 19 *et seq.*, 23 *et seq.*, 35, 37, 38, 40 *et seq.*, 55 *et seq.*, 69, 73, 78, 87 *et seq.*, 97, 106, 133, 135 *et seq.*, 141

Hall, Mr & Mrs Maurice, 6, 29, 31, 34, 69, 131, 133, 134
Hand-painted crests, 130
Harrison, J.F., 16, 37, 39, 40, 42, 55, 63, 97, 130, 136
Hill, A.J., 91
Ivatt, H.A., 20
Locomotive Exchanges (1925), 21
Locomotive Exchanges (1948) 144, 145
Locomotives, Gresley types;
 'A1' 4-6-2 *Great Northern*, 97 *et seq.*, 146
 'A4' 4-6-2, 36, 41, 56, 75, 104, 115, 123, 133, 143
 'B17' 4-6-0 (later 'B2'), 33, 51, 86 *et seq.*, 107, 148
 'D49/2' 4-4-0 (later 'D'), 87, 89, 148
 Garratt 2-8-8-2, 21, 65
 High pressure 4-6-2-2, 33
 'J39' 0-6-0, 107
 'J50' 0-6-0T, 87
 'K3' 2-6-0 (later 'K5'), 85 *et seq.*, 107
 'K4' 2-6-0 (later 'K1'), 33, 106 *et seq.*, 148, 150
 'P2' 2-8-2, 56 *et seq.*, 75, 87, 99, 136
 'V2' 2-6-2, 33, 35, 51, 69, 73 *et seq.*, 81, 87, 135, 144, 146
 'V4' 2-6-2, 51
Locomotives, other types:
 Holden 'B12' 4-6-0 (later 'B12/4'), 25, 93
 Ivatt 'D3' 4-4-0, 123, 130
 Paget locomotive, 13
 Raven 'B16' 4-6-0 (later 'B16/3'), 77 *et seq.*
 Raven electric traction, 19, 20
 Robinson 'B3' 4-6-0, 35
 Robinson 'J11' 0-6-0, 45, 47
 Robinson 'O4' 2-8-0 (later 'O1'), 65, 67, 89, 144-5
 Robinson 'Q4' 0-8-0, 42-3
Locomotives, Thompson types:
 'A2/1' 4-6-2, 69 *et seq.*, 146, 148
 'A2/2' 4-6-2, 56 *et seq.*, 143, 146
 'A2/3' 4-6-2, 7, 109 *et seq.*, 131, 136, 144, 146
 'B1' 4-6-0, 47 *et seq.*, 75, 79, 81, 89, 107, 109, 131, 144 *et seq.*, 149, 150
 'L1' 2-6-4T, 79 *et seq.*, 87, 89, 107, 137
 'Q1' 0-8-0T, 43, 89
Marlborough College, 7, 9 *et seq.*, 15
Matthews, Sir Ronald, 7, 22, 41, 42, 69, 131

McCosh, Andrew K., 69, 131
'Newton coach', 121, 122
Newton, Sir Charles, 121, 146
North Eastern Railway, 13, 16 *et seq.*, 27, 73, 77
Paget, (Sir) Cecil, 13, 14
Parker, L.P., 141
Peppercorn, A.H., 39, 103, 107, 111, 121, 131, 136 *et seq.*, 150
Raven, Guendolen, *see* Thompson, Mrs Guendolen
Raven, Norman, 14, 15, 22, 34, 71
Raven, Sir Vincent, 14 *et seq.*, 19 *et seq.*, 23, 27, 29, 73, 77
Renumbering Scheme (1946), 116 *et seq.*,
Richards, H.W.H., 38
Robinson, J.G., 19, 21, 43, 45, 61, 65
Rugby testing plant, 133
St David's School, Reigate, 10, 11
Shildon works, 5, 27, 28, 31, 119
Smeddle, R.A., 39, 73
Spencer, Bert, 39, 40
Stamer, Arthur C., 15 *et seq.*, 20 *et seq.*, 26, 27
Stanier, (Sir) William A., 21, 37, 41, 42, 139
Stockton & Darlington Centenary, 21, 22
Stratford works, 5, 13, 22 *et seq.*, 26, 73
Thompson, Francis, 10
Thompson, Francis Edward (father), 7, 15, 17
Thompson, Guy, 6
Thompson, Mrs Francis Edward (mother), 10, 22
Thompson, Mrs Guendolen (wife), 14 *et seq.*, 21, 31, 34
Thompson, Revd R.W., 10
Thompson's grouping of locomotives, 86
Thom, R.A., 34
Townend, Peter, 98, 99
Vitry-sur-Seine plant, 56, 133
Wedgwood, R.L., 21
Whigham, Walter K., 17
Whitelaw, William, 17, 23
Wintour, F.W., 21, 23
Woodhead tunnel accident, 61, 63
Woolwich Arsenal, 13, 17
Worsdell, Wilson, 13 *et seq.*
York works, 18, 20, 39, 135